voice branding

HOW TO

ALIGN

YOUR SPEECH,
LANGUAGE,
AND

VOICE SKILLS

WITH YOUR

PROFESSIONAL

GOALS

for

executive

leaders

"If you're ready to intentionally develop your own unique, authentic speech and voice brand so that you empower and differentiate yourself, then read this book immediately!"

LYNDA STUCKY

Voice Branding For Executive Leaders

A Lynda Stucky Book

Book Cover by Tracey Miller | www.TraceOfStyle.com
Publishing by Weston Lyon | www.WestonLyon.com
Edited by Lauren Cullumber

ISBN:1500606162
EAN-13: 978-1500606169

Disclaimer:

This book is dedicated to my family.

Acknowledgements

I'd like to thank the many people who made this book possible: To Weston Lyon, a great book advisor, my client and a good friend. His ideas were bigger than any I could have conceived and paid off well in the end. I learned so much, and this book would not have been possible without his guidance.

To my family, for giving me advice and for helping me with the research of voices on YouTube. This is a fun but distracting task of listening sometimes for hours for just the right voice.

To colleagues and friends who gave me emotional support while going through the book process. To Jana, my Webmaster, for so aptly taking care of my online needs.

Lastly, I'd like to thank my clients, who are the very reason I wanted to write this book in the first place.

Voice Branding For Executive Leaders

Table of Contents

READ THIS FIRST!

"Perceptions are reality."

This book is about perceptions associated with our speech, language, and voice skills. It is intended to bring awareness of the way our voices can brand us in positive or negative ways.

Our voices are powerful tools that can help influence and provide greater impact. We can choose to make changes in our speech and voice to convey our vision and our purpose.

This book will help you establish a personal/professional vision to be a leader in your environment by becoming aware of the perceptions associated with your speech, language, and voice skills and providing sometimes humorous examples from celebrities who demonstrate characteristics through their on-screen characters.

I have laid this book out for you into five easy-to-read sections. Each section will bring your attention to the matter at hand and provide you with actionable tips to help you create and develop the voice you so desperately want. Here is what we are going to cover:

In Section 1, you will become aware of the concept of "Vocal Branding." You'll learn what it is and how you can develop your voice to portray the image you desire.

In Section 2, you will see "The Nine Voice Characteristics that People Unknowingly Judge You On." Each characteristic is looked at on a continuum, so we can look at each end of the spectrum and see other people's perceptions around those types of voices. With each competency, a tip is provided to help you determine your own skill set; and in some cases, help you develop a skill. These tools are provided so that you can make changes to align the speech, language, and voice skills you have with your vision of how you want to sound and be perceived.

In Section 3, I will give you an additional three characteristics to help you become aware of what not to do…as well as tips on how to shape your voice so that you will be perceived as a true, polished professional.

They include:

1. Uptalk, an inflection that sounds like someone is asking a question while making a statement.

2. Excessive nasality, a problem in resonance; sounds like a person is speaking through the nose.

3. Glottal Fry, a vocal characteristic that occurs when good breath support is not present and sounds like a popping, crackling sound. It often occurs at the ends of sentences when the speaker's intonation drops to the bottom of his or her pitch range.

This section also provides a process for making changes in any behaviors that need to be changed.

In Section 4, I'll show you specific industry challenges that exist for the following groups: Senior Finance and Marketing Executives, Professional Speakers, IT/Software Developer Executives with a Foreign Accent, and Professional Athletes (media training).

Every industry has its own unique set of communication skills that are necessary to be effective. If you work in one of the four industries, then this is where you will want to spend some time. However, even if you don't work in one of these areas, I still suggest reading this section. The skills for these industries can still help you develop the voice that you want.

In Section 5, I'll share with you four case studies from four unique clients, who had problems associated with speech, language, and voice and who worked hard to successfully shape and develop their voices to accomplish their ultimate goals. The outcomes were life changing because of the self-confidence that was gained and the opportunities that were presented to them.

With that being said, this book is not about how you have to be or ought to be. It is a gentle reminder that perceptions exist which have been formed based on the way people experience their world. We should all strive to be authentic, and this book is a careful examination of your professional goals so that you can align your communication skills with the professional image that you want to project. It's not about changing who you are to fit some specified ideal but rather becoming who you want to be.

This book is not a recipe book to be the perfect communicator, either. Each of us has a uniqueness that should be preserved. Sometimes those unique and imperfect characteristics define us in positive ways. But they can also brand us in negative ways. This book helps bring awareness to characteristics so that you, the reader, can decide what is right for you.

This book is for the executive leader who wants to develop speech, language, and voice skills to become a more polished professional and achieve his or her goals. In addition, this book is meant for emerging leaders who are looking to develop skills that will increase their chances of moving up in an organization.

Making changes in your speech or voice behavior to reach personal or professional goals is not always easy and it is an evolving process. There are many subsets in communication to master. It takes time and practice. Get comfortable thinking that only one or two competencies can be mastered at a time. But once you master a few, you can move on to the next ones.

Knowing what to do and actually making it happen can be challenging. It depends on your ability to make changes (time may be a factor), your confidence level and your motivation. If you have high self-efficacy, or the belief that you have the power to reach a goal, you are more likely to achieve your goals. To strengthen your self-efficacy, set small, achievable goals. Success with smaller goals will improve your ability to change larger ones no matter what the goal you are trying to achieve.

Speech and voice skills are powerful tools that you can use to empower, differentiate yourself, and to brand *you*! That's wonderful news! Be intentional about developing your speech, language, and voice skills to the level that reflects who you are and how you want to be perceived so that you will be perceived authentically and positively.

Warm wishes,

Lynda Stucky

PS – I've also included a BONUS Section with voice-over artist Zach Hanks - who has casted, directed and voiced characters in nearly 80 video games including the hit franchises *World of Warcraft, Call of Duty, Mass Effect, Dragon Age, and Final Fantasy.*

He has a lot of perspective about creating the right vocal sounds to convey meaning in the messages he must relay to his audience. He also has extensive experience with public speaking and offers tips and techniques to help you. I think you'll really enjoy this unique bonus.

Section 1

Vocal Branding Through Speech, Language, and Voice Skills to Identify and Differentiate YOU!

In this section, you will begin to explore your values and your goals so that you can align them with the sound of the person and professional you want to become. It takes time to develop skills if changes are needed, and it may not be easy to do. But if you are clear about who you are and where you want to go, you can begin to examine your current brand and make the necessary changes to align your vocal image with that professional style.

"Everything you see or hear or experience in any way at all is specific to you. You create a universe by perceiving it, so everything in the universe you perceive is specific to you."

Douglas Adams, *Mostly Harmless*

Voice Branding

*"There's a wonderful phrase in psychology –
"the power of thin slicing"–which says that as
human beings we are capable of making sense
of situations based on the thinnest slice
of experience."*

Malcolm Gladwell, *Blink*

As a young woman entering into the work force for the first time, I was invited by my new employer to attend a professional development workshop on Team Building. This was one of those national seminars that traveled to different cities and employees from across the city attended. I did not know anyone attending and was pretty new to the workshop/seminar scene. When we arrived early that day we networked (which was really new to me) and sat together for breakfast. Then we were called together to get started. One of the first tasks that we were asked to do was to gather into small groups and appoint a leader. The chosen leader would then facilitate the group and be responsible for reporting the information we had discussed to the larger group.

We were pulled together in groups based on where we were sitting. Our first task to complete as a small group was to decide, "Who should be our leader of the group?" As I was sitting there looking around at my team and still thinking about who I thought might be a good leader, nearly everyone in my group pointed to me or said without any hesitation, "Lynda." I was completely surprised! I immediately thought, "Really?" and then wondered, "Why did they choose me?"

I had never thought of myself as a leader, nor had I ever thought about what characteristics a leader has. I barely knew these people. Prior to this workshop, I had never met anyone in my small group although I had talked to some of them briefly at the beginning of the day or at breakfast. How could they make a decision about me based on a few things that I had said and/or the way that I looked? That day, I was wearing a bright red jacket with a white turtleneck sweater and some costume jewelry—nothing really all that exciting. I was quite young (in my early 20s). I also felt emboldened because others saw something in me that I didn't recognize in myself and so my confidence grew instantly. I took my role for the day very seriously. Admittedly, I liked it; being a leader felt good! I felt a sense of pride for being chosen even if the role was merely facilitating the discussion. (I remember having this same feeling when I was chosen to be the line leader in kindergarten!)

At the same time that I felt honored and flattered, I was perplexed. Here I had been branded as a leader for an exercise based on very little information people had about me. And I was just as guilty of being judgmental. There were several people in our group whom I would have picked and several whom I considered "not appropriate" for the role. Since we all had very limited information about each other, it boiled down to two things:

1.) The "look"

2.) The "sound" we portrayed.

Whatever the definition of a leader meant at that time for that audience (the other participants at the workshop) was the image I portrayed. I was perceived as a leader based on their understanding and organization of sensory information (sight, sound) to represent and understand the environment they were in.

Here are three valuable lessons I learned that day:

1. People size each other up in very short amounts of time and with very little information about the other person.

> "All things are subject to interpretation. Whichever interpretation prevails at a given time is a function of power and not truth."
>
> **Friedrich Nietzsche**

2. Looking and sounding the part of a leader are important to being considered for new roles and responsibilities.

3. I felt differently about myself when people saw something different in me that was positive, even if I didn't see it myself.

What I wondered about after that exercise was what specific characteristics played a part in the decision of others to choose me. I was inspired and quickly felt a sense of responsibility to find out and to develop even further, so that I would look, sound and act like a leader.

Since I didn't know specifically what characteristics people saw in me that day, I started reading a lot more books on leadership characteristics. Through my reading, I discovered the phrase "perceptions are reality" by Lee Atwater. This sentence really struck a chord with me. I knew that there was a lot of truth to this because of my experience at the Team Building workshop.

My next strategy was to study and copy those people around me whom I deemed powerful leaders with executive presence and charisma. I watched how they carried themselves, how they spoke and looked and then tried to imitate them. There was growth in this area for me (it is important to watch others and begin collecting an inventory of styles) but what I was doing didn't always feel natural or come easy. I was uncomfortable speaking up in situations—my voice was shaky and shrill and it just didn't carry. I felt unnatural and inauthentic.

It wasn't until another Leadership workshop that my employer sent me to that I realized how wrong I was about the way I was doing things. At this workshop, we were encouraged to explore who we were as professionals and what was important to us. We delved into our values and personal mission statements. We collaborated with each other on the perceptions we had of others and how they matched or were mismatched with whom they appeared to be. For one activity, we were required to write down words/phrases that described what we valued and wished to communicate to people, even if we just met for the first time. It was through this exercise that I realized that the things that I valued (being humble, sincere, likeable) could be expressed through my speech, language, and voice skills as much as through a visual representation of me.

> "I don't want other people to decide who I am. I want to decide that for myself."
>
> **Emma Watson**

By understanding and verbalizing my values and what's important to me, I could begin to work on expressing them in everything that I do, including communication. It suddenly hit me for the first time that communicating authentically required this understanding of myself. And being a strong leader meant aligning those values with the way I communicated. If I didn't, my communication skills would suffer and it would be difficult to gain trust and credibility.

This also solved an issue that was bothering me a lot. My work as a speech and voice coach seemed superficial because it placed a strong emphasis on personal image. Teaching and coaching "image" work emphasizes the importance of being judged. This felt superficial and unimportant. After all, our perceptions are not always correct, and it is what's on the inside of us that matters the most.

But statistics about first impressions, such as the way people get hired and promoted and characteristics that reduce trust and credibility, are statistics that are real. Research shows that decisions are made quickly about people when it comes to first impressions. In a lecture on negotiation, Professor Deepak Malhotra, a professor in Negotiation, Organizations and Markets at the Harvard Business School, spoke to students about how your audience needs to like you before they will do business with you.

The Harvard Business School Club advises members in its employment seminars that people who interview generally decide who they **won't** hire within the first seven to 30 seconds.

"If you aren't managing your own professional image, others are," says Harvard Business School professor Laura Morgan Roberts.

Why wouldn't we want to achieve the very best that we can be if we have goals to achieve? If we are learning to intentionally live out our goals and our values, it is only natural to express them through the way we communicate. So that when we are judged, we know that we are genuine and we are expressing ourselves the way we want to. Judgment from others doesn't matter as long as our visual and auditory representation reflects and is aligned with the person we want to be. This gave me a new understanding and purpose for my work as an executive coach.

I found this quote that expands on "perceptions are reality." Deborah Shane (DeborahShaneToolBox.com) said that "IF perceptions are reality, then lead with authenticity."

I like the tone of this quote for two reasons.

1) It assumes that authenticity is important, and

2) It accepts that perceptions are here to stay, so we need to become aware of how people perceive us, but in an authentic way.

Being authentic means being clear about who we are and being true to ourselves. And once we know who we are, we can intentionally demonstrate our values in everything that we say and do. Our leadership style and the image that we project will be aligned.

> "Successful impression management can generate a number of important personal and organizational benefits, including career advancement, client satisfaction, better work relationships (trust, intimacy, avoiding offense), group cohesiveness, a more pleasant organizational climate, and a more fulfilling work experience. However, when unsuccessfully employed, impression

management attempts can lead to feelings of deception, delusion, preoccupation, distraction, futility, and manipulation." --Harvard Business School professor Laura Morgan Roberts, from an interview on "Creating a Positive Professional Image."

As I have evolved as a speech coach over the years, it has become clearer to me that the way we sound creates perceptions and influences the audiences we encounter. You have an identity, too, based on the way you sound and the way you look. It's a personal brand that you have available to use as a tool to market yourself, to persuade and influence and to create greater impact.

The way you speak indicates where you grew up and may quickly identify your level of education, personal tastes, and social background. Your personal brand differentiates you from everyone else. For example, you need only to say one or two words before someone can say, "Oh, that sounds like (your name)." Maybe your friend or colleague even says, "You sound tired today." If you were to hear a recording of a famous person (an actor, or our president, etc.) do you think that you could identify him or her after only a short phrase even if you didn't have a visual cue of the person? That is speech and voice branding.

> "We often try to be what others want us to be and in doing so, lose our own power. Connect your personality with your passion to create your purpose and make yourself powerful."
>
> **Unknown**

Leading in a very intentional way requires communication skills that match. Your speech, language, and voice are professional tools to showcase your values and help you achieve success! Your communication must always convey your vision, your purpose and your values in order to build credibility, be trustworthy and likeable, and ultimately achieve the professional goals you have set for yourself.

Awareness Exercise:

At the workshop that I referred to earlier, we did an interesting exercise of writing down three words that we would like people to say about us in relation to our professions (our desired perception). These three words were descriptive words that we wanted people to use to describe us as and remember us by.

Write down three adjectives that would describe who you are or who you want to be if people are talking about you. Here is a list of words to help you get started:

Friendly, authoritative, commanding, sincere, honest, mature, independent, professional, intellectual, confident, etc.

    1. _____

    2. _____

    3. _____

These three words should describe your interaction with others, express your core values and make you proud to be remembered in this way. Now, think about what a person with those descriptive words looks and sounds like.

For example, if you wrote down that you want to be remembered for being honest and sincere, what does that sound like to you? What does it look like?

If you are not sure, think of a person that you know who conveys honesty and sincerity. What speech, voice and language characteristics do they possess? Here is a list of words that are elements of speech, language, and voice that may help you identify outstanding characteristics.

Pitch - a perception of the highness or lowness of a vocal sound.

Volume - the intensity or loudness of a voice.

Nasality - the resonance of a voice that sometimes sounds like it comes from the nose (too much) or maybe sounds muffled (too little) if the person is suffering from a cold, or deep and full (just right).

Voice quality - the sound of the voice—could be clear, raspy, hoarse, breathy, etc.

Rate of speech - the speed at which a speaker talks.

Diction/pronunciation - the production of consonants and vowels.

Rhythm of speech - the cadence of speech—smooth, natural and fluent or halting, choppy, uneven.

Pitch variation - the intonation and inflection of pitch.

Grammar - the way we put sentences together (either standard or nonstandard).

Vocabulary - word usage.

Conciseness - how succinct and clear a speaker makes his/ her message.

It is a combination of these characteristics that make us each unique and we have the ability to manipulate them to create a sound. Often our body language adds to the perception, but we can determine a person's voice without visual cues.

If you really want to know how people perceive you, ask your family, friends, and colleagues that same question. Have them write down three words that describe you. Does your desired image match what the people around you say? If so, great! If not, there seems to be a gap.

According to the Center for Creative Leadership, "before you make any changes, be sure to get a good, truthful picture of your image. Take time to understand how others see you and why. Seek feedback from colleagues, your boss and direct reports. Ask your friends, children and significant other.

Each of these points of view will shed light on how your words and behavior are viewed by the people around you." Understand that this is a process that takes time and you won't have immediate results, but rarely are dramatic changes required. (Source: Building An Authentic Leadership Image Podcast.)

Take a minute to think about three people whose speech and voice you really like. Then think about three people whose speech and voice you don't like. Write them down.

Like

1. _____

2. _____

3. _____

Dislike

1. _____

2. _____

3. _____

What are the unique characteristics of each of these voices? (e.g. Low-pitched? Sexy? Shrill? Nasal? Rough?)

Normally, it's not just one characteristic that identifies a person but a combination of speech, language, and voice characteristics that when combined make a distinctive sound. And the sound that you hear often has a perception associated with it.

We often choose whom we talk to in new situations based on our perceptions of what we see and hear. We are hard-wired that way...our perceptions are based on how we know the world around us. It also serves well in the case of fight or flight. If I am judging others, then certainly others are judging me. What image do I convey? Is it positive or negative? Does it reflect the person whom I want to be? How can I be a visual and auditory representation of that person and still be authentic?

Explore your Speech and Voice Brand

As you think about your image and the impact you would like to have, what characteristics do you need to achieve that goal?

_____

_____

_____

_____

What would it mean for your career to enhance your leadership skills through your communication skills?

_____

_____

_____

_____

What would you gain from improving your communication skills?

_____

_____

_____

_____

In order to get to the place I want to be, I must sound:

_____

_____

_____

_____

> "I like the challenge of trying different things and wondering whether it's going to work or whether I'm going to fall flat on my face."
>
> **Johnny Depp**

Section 2

The Perceptions of Speech, Language, and Voice Skills That May Be Interfering With Your Leadership

In this section, I have divided speech, language, and voice skills into a set of nine competencies. Each of these is represented by a category (speech, language, or voice) and a subcategory of that category. Each of the competencies can be manipulated to a certain degree to create a sound. The competencies are discussed on a continuum. At each end of the continuum are extreme examples of the skill being overused or underused.

With the continuum of extreme behaviors listed on either end, common perceptions associated with that extreme competency are provided. Often times, an overused or underused competency has a negative perception associated with it. Under that, typical listener reactions are listed. Read these like you are the listener experiencing the speaker. You may add more of your own personal perceptions to the list if you think of some.

You may not always agree with the reaction. The same reactions can be felt at either end of the spectrum. For example, speaking with a small vocabulary can be condescending (if it is apparent that the speaker thinks that the listener isn't very bright) and speaking with too large of a vocabulary can also be condescending when the speaker uses that vocabulary to purposely talk over someone's head. Your task is to decide where on the continuum your desired speech, language, and voice skills need to be based on the values you wish to convey, the audience you are speaking to, and the personal style that makes you authentic and real.

At the end of each of the sub-categories, there is a tip for becoming more aware of your behaviors or a tip to change or eliminate a behavior. In many places, you will find additional resources online to refer to that are examples of the skill.

With each tip, you will have the opportunity to observe a celebrity demonstrate the characteristic that is being discussed. We can learn a lot from the actors who use their speech, language, and voice, often in unique ways, to convey the character they are portraying. To make their role believable, they must convey their character not only in their actions, but in their words and their voice. Look for "Celebrity Corner" to view the examples online.

When you see a "Celebrity Corner," you will also see a link. This link will take you to a site where you can listen to examples of the characteristic that was just discussed in that place of the book.

> "If we don't empower ourselves with knowledge, then we're gonna be led down a garden path."
>
> **Fran Drescher**

Category: Speech

Subcategory: Rate

Too Slow

←──

Perceptions of Speaker May Be:

- ☐ Slow thinking

- ☐ Not very bright

- ☐ Cautious and deliberate

- ☐ Unsure of himself/herself

Listener Reaction:

- ☐ May be thinking, "This is boring."

- ☐ May wish that the speaker would hurry up!

- ☐ May have a tendency to want to complete sentences for the speaker.

- ☐ The listener's mind may wander.

Category: Speech

Subcategory: Rate

Too Fast

Perceptions of Speaker May Be:

- ☐ Business-like

- ☐ Focused

- ☐ Tense/intense

- ☐ Hurried and impatient

Listener Reaction:

- ☐ May put listener on edge.

- ☐ May increase feelings of intensity.

- ☐ May not be able to understand the message.

- ☐ May be thinking, "Slow down!"

- ☐ May feel that the speaker "Doesn't have time for me."

Category: Speech

Subcategory: Rate

The first step is to determine (and have awareness of) your rate of speech. You will need a stopwatch or a clock with a second hand on it (or ask a partner to time you) to do this exercise. Read this paragraph quietly to become familiar with it.

Then time yourself reading the paragraph out loud to determine how fast you read. Read for one minute and mark the place where you end at one minute. Try to read this passage at the same rate that you speak in conversation. (Do not read the numbers in parenthesis out loud. This number represents the number of words up until that point.)

When the sunlight strikes raindrops in the air, they act as a prism and form a rainbow. The rainbow is a division of white light into many beautiful colors. These take the shape of a long round arch, with its path high above, and its two ends apparently beyond the horizon.

There is, according to legend, a boiling pot of gold at one end. People look, but no one ever finds it. When a man looks for something beyond his reach, his friends say he is looking for the pot of gold at the end of the rainbow.

Throughout the centuries people have explained the rainbow in various ways. Some have accepted it as a miracle without physical explanation.

To the Hebrews it was a token that there would be no more universal floods. The Greeks used to imagine that (140) it was a sign from the gods to foretell war (150) or heavy rain. (154) The Norsemen considered the rainbow as a (160) bridge over which the gods passed from earth to their (170) home in the sky.

Others have tried to explain the phenomenon physically (180). Aristotle thought that the rainbow was caused by reflection of (190) the sun's rays by the rain. Since then physicists have (200) found that it is not reflection, but refraction by the raindrops which causes the rainbows.

Many complicated ideas about the rainbow have been formed. The difference in the rainbow depends considerably upon the size of the drops, and the width of the colored band increases as the size of the drops increases. The actual primary rainbow observed is said to be the effect of super-imposition of a number of bows.

If the red of the second bow falls upon the green of the first, the result is to give a bow with an abnormally wide yellow band, since red and green light when mixed form yellow. This is a very common type of bow, one showing mainly red and yellow, with little or no green or blue.

(*The Rainbow Passage*, a public domain text, can be found on page 127 of the 2nd edition of Grant Fairbanks' *Voice and Articulation Drillbook.* New York: Harper & Row.)

Would you like to hear examples of different rates?

I set up a resource page for you to listen to the same passage being read at different rates. It will give you awareness of how pausing and lengthening vowels contributes to a slower pace. Compare the fastest and the slowest rates side-by-side. What differences do you hear in terms of vocal expressiveness and intonation? How do you feel listening to the different rates?

www.clearly-speaking.com/voice-branding-for-executive-leaders

A good rate of speech ranges between 140 -160 words per minute. A rate higher than 160 words per minute can make it difficult to absorb the material or understand the speaker. To slow your rate, lengthen the vowels, take more pauses (especially at punctuation) and try exaggerating your mouth movements as you speak. If you speak with a foreign accent, it is particularly important to slow down. Your listeners may be distracted by the sound of an accent. Controlling as many factors as possible will improve your intelligibility.

If you speak too slowly, you may need to speed up by saying your words and sentences faster. Possible causes for too slow a rate of speech include a regional drawl, a foreign accent or the model you had as a child. Non-native speakers may have slower rates because they are searching for the correct pronunciation or even looking for the right vocabulary.

As vocabulary and pronunciation improve, your rate of speech will also increase. To improve language abilities, take as many opportunities as possible to practice speaking with native speakers.

Whether you speak too quickly or too slowly, find your own passages to read and count the words to 160. Practice mastering the slower (or faster) reading rate to become aware of the way it feels and sounds to speak within that speech rate range. This is a necessity for carrying over the rate into your conversational speech.

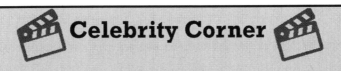

Celebrity Corner

Kramer (*Seinfeld* character)

If you would like to hear a humorous example of a fast rate of speech (induced by caffeine), go to the resource page to watch. Kramer drinks a little too much coffee and it has disastrous results on the way he speaks. Take note of how flat his speech sounds, and how muffled and difficult it is to understand his speech because his diction is so poor.

K-Billy's Super Sounds of the 70's

On the other end of the spectrum, you can hear a slow speaker. Unlike the speaker that is so fast that we are struggling to catch words, with the slow speaker, we grow impatient and tire easily of the time it takes to get the message across. Some people might want to finish the sentence for him.

www.clearly-speaking.com/voice-branding-for-executive-leaders

Category: Speech

Subcategory: Pronunciation and Diction

Sloppy, Imprecise

←——————————————————————————————————————

Perceptions of Speaker May Be:

☐ Uneducated

☐ Careless

☐ Informal

Listener Reaction:

☐ May think that the speaker is not credible.

☐ May have less impact.

☐ May find the speaker difficult to understand.

Category: Speech

Subcategory: Pronunciation and Diction

Precise

$\longrightarrow$

Perceptions of Speaker May Be:

- ☐ Educated

- ☐ Aristocratic

- ☐ Classy

Listener Reaction:

- ☐ May feel that the speaker is more formal.

- ☐ May think that the speaker is very professional.

- ☐ Will find the speaker easy to understand, and easy to listen to.

Category: Speech

Subcategory: Pronunciation and Diction

The acceptable pronunciation of any word is determined exclusively by its usage in the general population. But a dictionary can be a valuable tool to learn how to pronounce words. Pronunciation in the dictionary is represented by symbols of the International Phonetic Alphabet (IPA). If you're not familiar with IPA, each symbol in the IPA stands for one sound. This is different from our regular alphabet in which one symbol stands for many sounds. For instance, the sound /a/ can be produced as in bad, bade, and ball. Mastering the IPA system will assist you in many ways, particularly when you need to look up a word.

It is important to become aware of your speech patterns and determine your pronunciation. Record yourself reading a passage (see page 37, Rainbow Passage) and then listen to it. What mistakes are you making? Can you hear all the sounds in words? Are you saying word endings completely? Circle the words that give you problems. Read them out loud, making sure that every vowel and consonant is produced. Now read the paragraph again with the recorder on and make sure that every sound is clear and distinct. You may need to slow down to say every word clearly.

There are several types of common errors to listen for that, if spoken, make the sentence nonstandard. Here are a few common vowel and consonant mistakes:

The shortening of the vowel or consonant:	Interchanging letters or reversing two letters in a word:	Omitting sounds completely:	Adding sounds:	Saying sounds that are present in the word but not spoken:
"Our"= 'r' "R reservation is at 7:00."	Ask sounds like "axe" "Axe me a question."	"Picture"= "Pitcher" "That's a nice pitcher on your wall."	Across=Acrost	Calm=/l/ should be silent
"For"="fer" "The phone is fer you."	Escape=ekscape	"Probably"="Probly"	Interchange /t/ and /d/ "letter"="ledder" "quantity"="quanidy"	Balk=/l/ is silent
"To"="tuh" "I'm going tuh the store."	Children=childurn	Omitting /l/ "Already"="Awready"		Corps=/s/ should be silent
"Just"="jist" "Jist a minute..."	Perform=preform	"Didn't"="dint," "Wouldn't"="wunt"		Sword=/w/ is silent
"You"="ya" "Yer"= you are		Entertain=Enertain		Illinois=/s/ is silent
"Yes"="yeah" or "yup"		Friendly=Frienly		Subtle=/b/ is silent
"Going to"="gonna" "Want to"="wanna"		Contact=Contac		

What Can You Do to Ensure that You Pronounce Words Correctly?

- Put endings on words.

- Lengthen the vowels of stressed words.

- Over-articulate or exaggerate your sounds and words.

Errors can be corrected with commitment, determination, and daily practice.

For non-native English speakers, there may be sounds in the English language that do not exist in your native tongue. The omission of certain consonants is often alright so long as it doesn't affect intelligibility. But others, if missing, may drastically change the way a word is understood. The mispronunciation of vowels affects intelligibility the most. See a specialist to get an inventory of your speech sounds and to get advice on how much these sounds are interfering with intelligibility.

If you ever run across words that are difficult to pronounce and then you avoid using them because you are afraid you might mispronounce them, here is a systematic way to correct the problem:

1. Look up the word on www.dictionary.com and listen to the pronunciation.

2. Then imitate the word like you hear it.

3. Next, practice the new word by repeating it five times in a row.

4. Now make up sentences using the new word.

5. Finally, practice using the new word with familiar people. You will gain confidence each time you use the new word and soon it will be part of your everyday conversation.

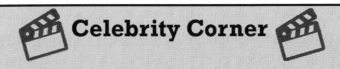
Celebrity Corner

Farmer Fran (*Waterboy* character)

On the resource page there is an exaggerated example of diction that is so poor that no one can understand the speaker. You can see that the listeners are left wondering and confused about what was just said. We may feel compelled to ask for clarification, but asking over and over again or straining to hear for long periods of time makes the listener weary. It is not uncommon for listeners to pretend to hear or dismiss the speaker entirely after a period of time.

I Love Lucy

Also, take a look at the clip about English Pronunciation with I Love Lucy. English pronunciation is difficult given all the different spellings for vowels and consonant combinations. It is a good idea to practice your presentation in front of someone before giving it just to make sure that you are pronouncing all the words correctly.

www.clearly-speaking.com/voice-branding-for-executive-leaders

Category: Speech

Subcategory: Rhythm

Choppy

←——————————————————————————————

Perceptions of Speaker May Be:

☐ Not credible

☐ Not polished

☐ Not from this region or country

Listener Reaction:

☐ May be distracted.

☐ May find it difficult to listen to.

☐ May tune out the message and focus on the distraction.

Category: Speech

Subcategory: Rhythm

Natural, Smooth

Perceptions of Speaker May Be:

☐ Fluent

☐ Polished

☐ Fluid

Listener Reaction:

☐ Will believe that the speaker is respectable.

☐ Will sound credible.

☐ Will be influential.

Category: Speech

Subcategory: Rhythm

The two most frequent problems associated with rhythm are:

1) The presence of word fillers, and

2) The use of a cadence that is different from American English.

Word fillers take many shapes and forms:

> "uh," "um," "so," "you know what I mean," "and," "ok?", "right?", "like," etc.

If used too frequently, they become distractions to your overall message.

A colleague told me that he went to hear a speaker at a seminar but he was unable to tell me what the speaker talked about. The speaker had so many "uhs" in his speech that the entire table where my friend was sitting began counting them with slash marks on a sheet of paper.

By the end of the presentation, none of participants at the table could tell what was discussed. The speaker's message was not heard and his credibility about being an expert in that topic had disappeared!

You must first determine how often you use word fillers and in what situations. Ask a friend to count the number of word fillers you use in one minute. Your friend should watch the time and count your fillers in the following situations (talk for one minute on each topic):

1. Talk about yourself.

2. Talk about any subject that you are passionate about.

3. Respond to a question on a topic that you are less familiar with. Give your opinion about that topic.

Respond in one minute and then stop. Count the number of fillers and types of fillers used. How many fillers did you use in each situation?

If in one minute, you used more than three, try to eliminate them altogether or bring the number down to below three per minute. Many people use word fillers in certain situations/ topics that are more stressful. Do you?

Learn to substitute silence in those places where you are tempted to insert a word filler. Practice and try the exercise again. Can you reduce the number of word fillers? Practice this exercise again to continue to reduce the number of word fillers. Don't substitute a new word filler (e.g. "and" or "so" in place of "um"). Be sure that you are inserting silence where you pause.

Avoid sounding like you are hesitating when pausing. Your pause can be an effective and powerful tool to create emphasis and drama. There is not a standard number for the frequency you pause but the pause should contribute to the effect. Pausing (with silence) at punctuation is a great place to start.

A *cadence problem* is often related to the way words are stressed and whether there is a smooth transition between words. A non-native speaker often uses the cadence of his native tongue and transfers it to the second language. Some languages have a more staccato sounding cadence that gives equal length to every syllable. Of course, in English we lengthen our stressed syllable vowels. This staccato sounding speech is often described as rapid fire and halting. It is often extremely difficult to understand for native speakers especially if it is accompanied by a fast rate of speech.

A non-native English speaker may not know where to place the syllable stress of a word. Having someone help you with this can be very helpful. Take an inventory of all the longer words that you say within your work setting. These are the words that you frequently say with your colleagues and customers. Look through your department literature and the emails that you receive. You should be able to come up with a list of 100 or more words.

Once you have a list, go through it again and look for multi-syllable words. Say the list of words to a native speaking friend. Have him or her correct the words that you mispronounce. Circle them and listen carefully to the way your friend says them. Try to repeat those words just the way that you heard them. Record yourself saying the list of words. You should be able to read a list quickly and correctly without thinking about how to say the words. Next, say the word and make up a sentence using the word. Can you still pronounce it correctly in a sentence? If not, work on the sentences.

When making up sentences, be sure to make up sentences that are relevant to your work setting. Sentences should be ones that you would actually say in a conversation.

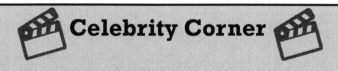

Celebrity Corner

There are some examples of the different types of rhythm problems on the resource page that may undermine credibility and distract the listener to the point that the message is completely lost.

Milton from *Office Space*
Listen to the short, choppy words that give the speech a staccato sound. Words are cut short and are abrupt.

Also, go to the resource page to hear a few non-native English speakers whose rhythm of speech is significantly different from the American English's rhythm. Some accents sound more disjointed and halting. The cadence is not smooth, natural or fluent. Since we are used to hearing the American English rhythm, we often don't easily process another language's rhythm. See if you can identify the rhythm differences.

Clueless
Perhaps more common to a younger, youthful speaker is the use of "like." You can hear it on the clip of a woman talking in the movie *Clueless*.

www.clearly-speaking.com/voice-branding-for-executive-leaders

Category: Language

Subcategory: Grammar

Use of Non-Standard English

←————————————————————————————————————

Perceptions of Speaker May Be:

☐ Uneducated

☐ Not from the region

☐ Non-native speaker

Listener Reaction:

☐ May diminish speaker's credibility.

☐ May find it hard to understand.

☐ May find the non-standard speech
a distraction.

Category: Language

Subcategory: Grammar

English Expert

Perceptions of Speaker May Be:

- ☐ Aristocratic

- ☐ Educated

- ☐ Professional

- ☐ Stiff or stuffy

Listener Reaction:

- ☐ May feel intimated/inadequate.

- ☐ May feel uncomfortable/comfortable.

- ☐ May be impressed.

Category: Language

Subcategory: Grammar

On the grammar spectrum, grammar and word usage may largely be dependent upon the audience. That is why the listener reaction could be two opposite reactions. Here are some tips:

1. Adjust your grammar (informal vs. formal) to fit your audience. Learn to loosen up your speech when you need to but tighten it in high stakes/high visibility situations.

2. If you are regularly using non-standard English, find out your mistakes and correct them. Mistakes are often associated with a regional dialect of English or with foreign accents. Write out the sentences you use and the corrected sentences. Review your list frequently.

Common Mistakes to Avoid:

- Use of words that are not real words, e.g. "Irregardless"

- "Lay" and "lie" are often used synonymously. "I want to lie down" is correct.

- The use of "should of" vs. "should have." "I should have gone with him" is correct.

- The use of "good" vs. "well." "I am doing well" is correct.

- The use of "who" vs "whom." "You are talking to whom?" is correct.

- Inappropriate preposition usage. "Where is she at?" is incorrect, "Where is she?" is correct.

- Wrong relative pronoun usage. "This is the woman that lived in Australia" is incorrect, "This is the woman who lived in Australia." is correct.

- Subject/verb agreement is wrong. "There's six agenda items to discuss." vs. "There are six agenda items to discuss." The latter is correct.

Frequent Mistakes Used by High-Level, Non-Native English Speakers:

- Omission of endings, especially plurals and past tense endings

- Omission of articles (a, an, the)

- Subject/verb agreement

- Pronouns—incorrect gender/number

- Prepositions are misused

- Relative pronouns (who, whom; that, which)

- Modals (these add meanings like ability, permission, obligation)

Every language has common grammar errors associated with it. It is recommended that you contact a certified specialist (speech pathologist, linguist, ESL instructor) to get a full inventory of the errors that you may be making in your speech. Even though non-native English speakers are often highly educated and can speak multiple languages, grammar mistakes are <u>perceived</u> as the speaker being uneducated. If you are looking for a great book to help you out, I recommend *Errors in English and Ways to Correct Them* by Harry Shaw (4th Edition, Harper and Row). This book provides quick answers to simple grammatical questions. In my experience, most non-native English speakers know the rules and the correct ways but just forget to use them.

When it comes to appearing to be competent, articulate and qualified, even small changes can boost your potential for business success. Speaking well may influence the listener as to whether or not he wants to pursue a business relationship with you.

Category: Language

Subcategory: Vocabulary/Word Choice

Too Simple

←————————————————————————————

Perceptions of Speaker May Be:

- ☐ Uneducated

- ☐ Not very bright

- ☐ Simple-minded

- ☐ Not experienced

- ☐ Immature

Listener Reaction:

- ☐ May feel the message is boring.

- ☐ May not want to pay attention.

- ☐ May feel speaker is not credible.

Category: Language

Subcategory: Vocabulary/Word Choice

Too Hard

Perceptions of Speaker May Be:

☐ Out-of-touch with the audience

☐ Superior

☐ Intelligent

Listener Reaction:

☐ May feel uncomfortable.

☐ May be bored and lost.

☐ May tune out the message.

☐ May feel like the speaker is being condescending.

Category: Language

Subcategory: Vocabulary/Word Choice

Audience is everything! Knowing who you are talking to is the best metric of knowing what vocabulary you need to use. Study your audience carefully to find out what appeals to them, and what words they will respond to. The following list has attributes you may want to consider:

- Gender

- Age

- Social or Economic class

- Education level

- Technical knowledge

- Culture

Since the goal is to appeal to your listener, be sure to consider their values and background. Use simple language when talking to most audiences. Resist the tendency to use industry words (unless you are speaking to those in that industry) or big fancy words. Use simple words to convey your message precisely.

Here are some other tips:

Use Positive Words

Words like assure, transform, can, will do, imagine, reform, courage, and restore are all words that shine positively. The way in which we deliver those words also influences. Convey a tone of confidence and comfort by lengthening vowels and taking long pauses to deliver a speech that is unhurried. Also use vocal variety to hold interest and convey an open, friendly discourse.

Use "You-Focused" Messages Frequently

"You-focused" language means that you are speaking to the listener and addressing his/her needs. It means understanding and empathizing with the other person (or the audience). This is a great way to connect with your audience. After all, it is all about them! Here are some examples of phrases to start with:

- You'll see...

- You'll discover...

- You will be...

When you use "you-focused" messages, it will sound and feel like you are having a conversation with your audience.

Strong vs. Weak language

Malcolm Goodale writes in *The Language of Meetings* (Language Teaching Publication) that using the word "would" in statements often creates a tone of tentativeness and eliminates the dogmatic tone. Here are some examples:

- I prefer to meet at 8:00 a.m. vs. I would prefer to meet at 8:00 a.m.

- The memo is too late. vs. The memo would be too late.

- That is unacceptable. vs. That would be unacceptable.

Various communication instances may require a dogmatic tone but other times, it is more socially acceptable to be tentative. Can you think of examples when this would be true? (Or, if you prefer...Can you think of examples when this is true?)

Changing a few words in a sentence can make a big difference in making a stronger statement. The following pairs of sentences relay the same message, but one is more effective. Which one sounds more powerful?

I have a problem with Joe--he's always late.
Joe has a problem--he is always late.

I think the solution lies in outsourcing the work.
The solution lies in outsourcing the work.

The candidate has been considered carefully.
He considered the candidate carefully.

The second statement in each pair is stronger. Resist starting statements with "I" (unless talking about yourself), eliminate hedging (e.g. "I think") and avoid using passive voice.

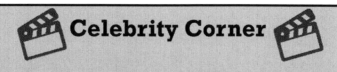

Celebrity Corner

When considering vocabulary to use with any audience, you can consider things such as age differences, gender differences, technical/industry understanding, etc. In the advertisement on the site, there is a clear disparity between the vocabularies of two generations.

Don LaFontaine GEICO spot.
In this example you can hear how the same message can be said in two different ways.

Under what conditions would the vocabulary that you use with your audiences need to change? Write down all the audiences that you speak to and then think of one concept you would like to explain to each audience. Would you say it differently depending on the audience?

	Audience	**Concept/Explanation**
1.		
2.		
3.		
4.		

www.clearly-speaking.com/voice-branding-for-executive-leaders

Category: Language

Subcategory: Conciseness of Speech

TMI (Too Much Information)

◄───

Perceptions of Speaker May Be:

☐ Scattered and disorganized

☐ The appearance of self-importance

☐ Not polished

☐ Decreased self-confidence

Listener Reaction:

☐ May wonder what the point is.

☐ May lose the message completely.

☐ May become annoyed and tune out the speaker.

☐ May feel that the speaker is not credible.

Category: Language

Subcategory: Conciseness of Speech

Minimalist

Perceptions of Speaker May Be:

- [ ] A hoarder of information

- [ ] Unsure and lacking self-confidence

- [ ] Not influential

- [ ] A loner

Listener Reaction:

- [ ] May feel that the speaker isn't a part of the team (or doesn't want to be).

- [ ] May leave the conversation guessing about the person's message.

- [ ] May feel demotivated to contribute.

Category: Language

Subcategory: Conciseness of Speech

If you talk too much, talk less and learn how to actually say more (with less). The ability to craft a message that stays on target is essential for effective communication and effective leadership. You must be absolutely clear and intentional about the point that you want to make and then add 1-3 supporting points. Also, practice responses that are no more than 30 seconds long.

Here are some topics...Use these to practice giving your opinion in a response that is 30 seconds long. Eliminate the details you feel compelled to say. (Let your audience ask you for more information.)

- The difference between having your own business and working for someone else.

- The best/worst political party (an interesting challenge for 30 seconds).

- The advantages/disadvantages of having a passport.

- Global warming.

Be sure to time yourself and don't go one second over 30 seconds. If this is too difficult, write out your message first to see excess wordiness. Then cut the response down.

This exercise of limiting words or sentences can be effective practice for saying more with less. It requires laser focus! As an even more challenging exercise, cut additional information and bring the response down to 15 seconds.

If you need to speak up more, practice giving your opinion more often. Share with others so that they are aware of what you are thinking. Compose messages (your opinion) about the topics listed or on something else. Then practice giving your opinion to someone else.

Informing appropriately is also audience-sensitive. Be aware of your audience's sophistication, receptiveness, timeliness of the message, and interest level.

> "As you grow in this business, you learn how to do more with less."
>
> **Morgan Freeman**

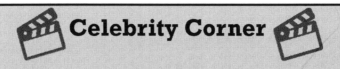

Celebrity Corner

The Internship

In this excerpt of a job interview, go back to the perceptions of a speaker who gives too much information. Although very funny in this example, giving too much information and not being concise with the message is a problem that significantly takes away from the message.

By the end of a conversation with someone who can't make a point concisely, the point - and the question - are completely misunderstood. Clarity of thought is crucial with a balance of detail.

www.clearly-speaking.com/voice-branding-for-executive-leaders

Category: Voice

Subcategory: Pitch

Too Low

Perceptions of Speaker May Be:

☐ Authoritative

☐ Commanding

☐ Influential

☐ Sounds like a man

*There is not a negative perception with a low pitch. Most people wish they spoke at a lower pitch! But, if you try to speak at a lower pitch and it is unnatural, you can actually damage your vocal cords and develop hoarseness. This will create a less desirable sound such as glottal fry. See the bonus section for more information about glottal fry.

Listener Reaction:

☐ May feel inclined to think that the speaker is credible.

☐ May believe that the speaker is sophisticated.

☐ May like the "sexy" sound of a low-pitched voice.

☐ May mistake speaker for the wrong gender.

Category: Voice

Subcategory: Pitch

Too High

Perceptions of Speaker May Be:

- ☐ Sounds feminine (if male)

- ☐ Child-like (if female)

- ☐ Speaker is young and immature

- ☐ If the speaker is male, he may frequently be confused as a female speaker.

- ☐ Shrill and abrasive

Listener Reaction:

- ☐ May not feel that the speaker is credible

- ☐ May feel annoyed if the voice is shrill

- ☐ May turn off listening and avoid conversations

- ☐ May mistake speaker for wrong gender

Category: Voice

Subcategory: Pitch

Do you know where your vocal pitch lies on the pitch range that you have? Your vocal cords operate optimally about ¼ of the way up from the bottom of your entire pitch range. (Your entire pitch range is the lowest note you can make all the way up to the highest note.)

This is the optimal place where you should speak to avoid problems with your voice. For some people, the habitual pitch (the pitch used most often) is not the optimal pitch. There are two ways to determine your optimal pitch.

These methods of listening to your pitch assume that you have a good ear and can detect pitch in your voice and match it to a tone. If you are unable to do this, ask a friend to help you.

Method 1:

Here is a simple exercise to determine if you speak at your optimal level of your range. Very simply, answer the following questions out loud with "uh-huh" and listen to where your pitch level is:

- Is sugar sweet?

- Are lemons sour?

Your pitch with that response is very close to where you should be habitually speaking. Say "uh-huh" again and start counting to 20 immediately afterwards. ("Uh-huh. 1, 2, 3, …")

Can you hear if you are staying at the same pitch that you said "uh-huh" while counting? You should be! That's where your pitch should be in conversation. If it is higher or lower than that place on your range, you may need to make some changes.

Method 2:

If you are good at matching your pitch at a piano, here is more precise way of determining your pitch.

Start at the very lowest pitch you can make and match that tone on the piano. Then, slide up to the highest pitch you can make. Match that tone on the piano. This is your range from lowest to highest.

A pitch range from lowest to highest notes on a piano.

Count the number of keys between your highest and lowest pitches. Then divide that number by four. In the example below, there are 26 keys in this person's range. (Remember to count both black and white keys).

Now divide 26 by 4. This equals 6.5. This means that the optimal pitch for this person is between 6 and 7 keys from the bottom of the range.

The number of keys between lowest and highest notes is 26.

Starting at the bottom of your range, count up the scale with the number of keys. That should be ¼ of the way up from the bottom. In the example above, count 6-7 keys up from the bottom.

*After dividing 26 by 4 to get 6.5, count up from the bottom of
the range 6 or 7 keys. This is the optimal pitch for this person.*

This is where this person's speaking voice should hover. Tap
the key and begin speaking. Your voice should match closely
to that pitch (with some variation since you are using intonation).

Most of us do not have a low-pitched voice like James Earl
Jones. The next best thing is to make sure that your habitual
pitch is at the optimal level, so you don't damage your vocal
cords, and then implement other strategies for a richer,
deeper sound. How? By using a wide-open mouth and exaggerated mouth movements (see page 96 for an exercise), and
by staying relaxed. These are the best ways to speak at the
optimal level and still command a room.

Our vocal cords pull together by the muscles around the larynx and when these muscles are tense it affects the tension and corresponding sound. The muscles of the larynx need to be tension-free to perform optimally. Imagine holding a clenched fist for a period of time. When you were ready to pick up a pencil or other object, the muscles of your hand would be stiff and tired for a while even for a simple act like picking up a pencil.

Vocal tension has the same effect. The muscles around the larynx are very susceptible to tension and if the muscles become tight, it will affect the vocal sound: you may have difficulty projecting your voice, the resonance may sound different, and the pitch may sound shrill. It may also be hard to breathe correctly with tension. The muscle groups that affect your vocal sound include the muscles of the neck, shoulders, and jaw.

Your problem may not be tension due to stress but rather tension associated with sitting at the computer monitor all day. Whatever the reason, being aware of your tension and then having strategies to improve are essential.

> "Voices are like fingerprints, from Cagney to Bogart. They never lost it. My voice is instrumental in categorizing me."
>
> **Sylvester Stallone**

If there is one thing that you could do to really improve the sound of your voice it would be to maintain a relaxed state. Since tension along the vocal tract creates a shrill, high-pitched tone, it is important to be relaxed. Here are some relaxation exercises to help you maintain a relaxed state:

Shoulders Exercise #1

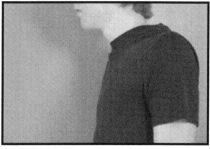

1. Lift your shoulders up and back; hold.

2. Tilt your head forward

3. Rock it from side-to-side. Don't turn your chin. Relax.

Shoulder Exercise #2:

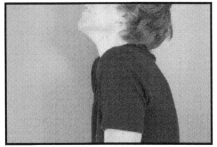

1. Lift your shoulders up and back; hold.

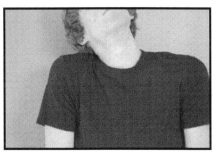

2. Rock your head from side-to-side.

Back of Neck Stretch:

1. Tilt your head forward with your chin on your chest.

2. Clasp your hands and rest them on the crown of your head.

3. Exert gentle pressure on the head and hold for five seconds.

Jaw Massage:

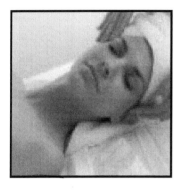

1. Begin at the cheekbone, massage in a small circular motion downward until you reach the lip line.

Larynx Exercise:

Hum up and down the scale or to your favorite relaxing music.

Nerves are the culprit for many speech and voice problems because the typical response to being nervous is that our muscles tense up and we take short, shallow breaths. Other problems include:

- A fast rate of speech

- Poor articulation/diction

- An inability to project

- A shrill, high-pitched sound

- Flat, uninteresting speech

- An increase in the number of word fillers

These simple exercises yield maximum benefit! Use these relaxation exercises every time you have to speak or present as a warm up, especially if you are nervous.

"Speech is one of the major methods of communication. Most of us have a voice but not everyone knows how to use it. You don't need to be a performer, a poet, or a politician to have a good voice: whatever your background, you will want your voice to be clear, resonant and free of tension so that your message is expressed intelligibly, audibly and engagingly."

Rebecca Root, Voice and Speech Teacher/Actor

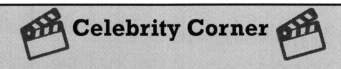

Celebrity Corner

When identifying a person's voice, we often think of the pitch of their voice. There are other characteristics that help as well, like the quality of voice, volume and resonance, but pitch is often immediately identifiable. (This person speaks high or low.) As you listen to the clips on the resource page, listen to them with your eyes closed.

1. Do you know who it is?

2. What is the distinguishing characteristic behind the voice?

3. If you don't know the voice or the actor, do you have a mental picture of the person?

4. If you do know the actor, does this person's voice fit the way that they look?

www.clearly-speaking.com/voice-branding-for-executive-leaders

Category: Voice

Subcategory: Loudness

Too Soft

←─────────────────────────────────────

Perceptions of Speaker May Be:

☐ Lacks self-confidence

☐ Shy

☐ Unsure

☐ Sexy

Listener Reaction:

☐ May feel they have to listen harder.

☐ May stop listening after multiple
requests to repeat.

☐ May feel frustrated.

*"Speech is a very important aspect of
being human. A whisper doesn't cut it."*

James Earl Jones

Category: Voice

Subcategory: Loudness

Too Loud

Perceptions of Speaker May Be:

☐ Overly confident

☐ Boisterous and aggressive personality

☐ Disregard for others

☐ Brash and arrogant

Listener Reaction:

☐ May be seen as seeking attention.

☐ May be annoying.

☐ May want to avoid that person.

Category: Voice

Subcategory: Loudness

If you speak too loudly, you may be dominating the conversation. Learn to listen more than you talk and when you do speak, you will effectively get your audience's attention. If you speak too quietly, people tire of requesting repeats and may disregard or interrupt you.

Become familiar with a loudness scale. Gauge your loudness on a scale from 1-10 with 10 being the very loudest that you can get. Where are you currently? Try to keep your conversational volume at around 3 on that scale.

A lack of projection is a significant problem that many people face. If you struggle with loudness, get comfortable practicing at least five different loudness levels with the following audiences:

1. One-on-one in a small office—normal conversation

2. One-on-one in a noisy restaurant/bar

3. 5-10 people in a small conference room

4. 10-30 people in a large conference room

5. Over 30 people in an auditorium

Don't let your pitch rise when speaking louder, and use amplification with more than 30 people. Work at sustaining the proper loudness levels in a variety of settings.

Exaggerate Your Mouth Opening When You Speak.

Think of your vocal tract as a megaphone that begins at the small opening of the vocal cords and opens up wider and wider so that your mouth is the end of the megaphone. The wider the mouth opening, the better the sound will carry out of your mouth.

You can see and hear a video of James Earl Jones and Malcolm McDowell, who demonstrate exaggerated mouth movements on a Sprint commercial.

Here is a simple exercise you can try to hear the difference. Grab a sheet of paper and roll it up into a tube. At one end, speak into the tube. Pay attention to the sound.

Next, roll the paper into a cone shape. It should look like a megaphone. Speak into one end again and note the way that it sounds compared to speaking into a tube. You can make the same comparison with your mouth. Keep your mouth clenched and barely open and then count to 20 out loud.

*Open your mouth wide to project
your voice like this megaphone.*

Next, open and exaggerate your mouth movements and count to 20 again. How does the sound differ?

Good Breath Support Is Essential

Good breath support is essential when it comes to voice projection and maintaining good vocal health. To test whether your air supply is sufficient, take a deep breath and sustain an /s/ sound (SSSSSS) for as long as possible while timing yourself. Women over the age of 16 should be able to sustain an /s/ for 15 seconds or more and men over the age of 16 should be able to sustain for 20 seconds or more. If you can't hold the /s/ this long and you don't have a medical respiratory problem, you need to practice breath control for speech.

(*Source: Manual of Voice Therapy, Rex J. Prater and Roger W. Swift, Little, Brown and Company, 1984.*)

Learn to Breathe Correctly

Learn to breathe correctly using the diaphragm muscle to get the best support for your vocal cords.

To gain awareness of appropriate breathing patterns, start in a supine position lying on your back on a firm mattress, or on the floor. Place your hand or a book on your abdomen directly under your rib cage. Inhale through the nostrils and as you breathe in, observe how your stomach and the book rise.

When you breathe out, your stomach and the book descend. The book should rise and fall in a smooth, rhythmic pattern.

That is it! Now all you have to do is make sure you are breathing like that while speaking, both sitting and standing.

Good breath support requires that you have great posture, so be sure that you are standing and sitting tall with your shoulders pulled back, and not slouching or slumping!

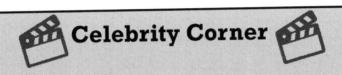

Celebrity Corner

On the resource page you can listen to a couple of humorous examples of the effects on the listener when the volume is too low. Watch how the listeners have to strain to hear and their reactions are often frustration.

As you listen, think about what loudness level you prefer. What situations call for a loud voice and what situations call for a softer volume in your work setting?

www.clearly-speaking.com/voice-branding-for-executive-leaders

Category: Voice

Subcategory: Expressive Intonation

Too Flat (Underused)

←———————————————————————————————

Perceptions of Speaker May Be:

☐ Not polished

☐ Not credible

☐ Unengaged

☐ Unfriendly

Listener Reaction:

☐ May find the speaker boring.

☐ May have difficulty listening.

☐ May be difficult to understand.

Category: Voice

Subcategory: Expressive Intonation

Too Much (Overused)

Perceptions of Speaker May Be:

☐ Insincere

☐ Overly-friendly

☐ Dishonest

☐ Over-the-top

Listener Reaction:

☐ May feel the speaker cannot be trusted.

☐ May think that speaker is not credible.

☐ May feel that speaker is hypocritical.

Category: Voice

Subcategory: Expressive Intonation

Lacking vocal expressiveness is a common problem. Sounding monotone won't captivate your audience. Here is a solution to help you become more vocally expressive:

Expressive individuals use a wide range of pitch variation in the message. Many people don't realize how much pitch they have available to them. The first step towards improving expressiveness is to become aware of your pitch range and become comfortable using it!

1. Start by imitating the sound of a siren. Say "ah" and start low in pitch and move slowly up as high as you can go. Once you are as high as you can go, come back down still saying "ah." Take a breath as you need to. Repeat this activity over and over again. This entire range is what is available to you in speech. You can stretch this range with practice.

2. Next, try counting while producing the siren sound. Count out loud while moving up and down with your voice.

3. Say your name and address while producing the siren.

4. Read material (a book, newspaper, children's books, etc.) while exaggerating your pitch. Try to use as much pitch range as you can even though this is not the way you would speak in a conversation. The point is to help you become comfortable. Record yourself if you can.

5. As you become comfortable with using more pitch, start using more variation of pitch in conversational speech. Use phone conversations as your first place to concentrate on incorporating more pitch variation. Record your end of the conversation, if you can, and then listen back to the recording to see if you changed your vocal pitch adequately. Monitor what words you stressed with pitch changes. Did you end sentences with falling pitch and questions with rising pitch at the end of the sentences? Speak slowly to accomplish adding variation.

If you are too expressive, try to hold back on flowery pitch changes. You want to be colorful but not dramatic (unless you are auditioning for a role in a play!)

If you follow this plan, you will be well on your way to developing vocal expressiveness and becoming fascinating to listen to!

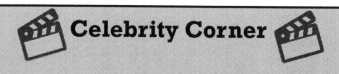

Celebrity Corner

Elaine Benes and David Puddy (*Seinfeld* Characters)

Listen to this example of very flat speech vs. very expressive speech. Elaine Benes (Julia Dreyfus) and David Puddy (Patrick Warburton) on *Seinfeld* engage in a conversation that shows extreme examples of being monotone vs. being very expressive.

Ellen Degeneres in *Finding Nemo*

Another example shows the youthfulness of expressive intonation. This may have a positive or a negative impact on speech. It depends on the situation. Do you ever need to be expressive like Dory in the executive world?

www.clearly-speaking.com/voice-branding-for-executive-leaders

Section 3

Common Characteristics That You Must Avoid If You Want to Sound like a Leader!

In this section, I have provided an additional three characteristics that don't really fit neatly on a continuum. But they are equally as important as any of the other characteristics already discussed because if you are talking with any of these characteristics, your credibility is suffering. They include "Uptalk" (inflection that sounds like one is asking a question while making a statement), excessive nasality (speaking through your nose), and glottal fry (a vocal characteristic that sounds rough and crackly and happens when you are speaking at the bottom of your pitch range). This section also provides you with a process for making changes when behaviors need to be adjusted.

"The limits of my language mean the limits of my world."

Ludwig Wittgenstein

Category: Voice

Subcategory: Inflection

Uptalk (Ending Sentences Like Questions)

Perceptions of Speaker May Be:

☐ Not confident

☐ Doubtful about the message

☐ Child-like

Listener Reaction:

☐ May feel that speaker is not trustworthy.

☐ Speaker doesn't sound credible.

☐ Speaker is young and immature.

Category: Voice

Subcategory: Inflection

Statements have more impact when they end with downward inflection. But when we ask questions, our pitch sometimes rises at the end. Use vocal inflection that demonstrates matter-of-fact confidence to inspire and persuade others.

To find out if you speak with uptalk, record your end of a phone conversation with your boss, a colleague, and then a friend in which you explain something. Listen to the recording after you have spoken to each person. Listen for the rising vocal pitch at the end of sentences. If it sounds like you are asking a question, you need to learn to make the same statements with a dropping vocal pitch.

Write down the sentences where you used uptalk and then record yourself intentionally using the dropping vocal inflection at the end. Notice how much stronger you sound when you make statements with downward inflection!

For some people, it is very difficult to hear these differences and make the necessary changes. If you have been told that you are using uptalk, enlist the help of a friend (or better yet, the person who first noticed this tendency in your speech) to assist you in making the needed changes. If you are unsure of what uptalk sounds like, I have recorded some audio for you to listen to. Go to the resource page to listen:

www.clearly-speaking.com/voice-branding-for-executive-leaders

Category: Voice

Subcategory: Resonance

Hypernasality (Too Much Nasality)

Perceptions of Speaker May Be:

☐ Boisterous

☐ Whiny personality

☐ Overly confident

Listener Reaction:

☐ May feel that speaker is too loud and shrill.

☐ Speaker is annoying.

☐ Speaker is difficult to listen to.

Category: Voice

Subcategory: Resonance

Some people sound more nasal when they speak. The resulting sound is a loud, shrill vocal quality. If you suspect you might speak through your nose, you can test it by placing your fingers on the bridge of your nose while saying the following sentence:

"The red bird had a loud chirp."

If you feel any nasal vibration along your nose, you are speaking through your nose. Since this sentence contains no nasal sounds, there should not be any vibration. If there is, you have too much nasality and you may need to learn how to lift/strengthen the soft palate in the back of the throat to close off the nasal passage.

There are three nasal sounds in English: /m/ as in mat, /n/ as in night and /ng/ as in sing. Every time you say a word with one of these sounds in it, your soft palate in the back of your throat drops down to allow the air to pass through the nose. For all other vowels and consonants, the soft palate, or velum, lifts up and closes off that nasal passage. For some people, the palate is "lazy" and doesn't lift. (There may also be physical reasons that cause the palate to drop down.) Train your palate by saying "ah" and holding it. Watch (in a mirror) how it moves in the back of your throat. It should be closing off. Go through all the vowels in the same way. If you are able to accomplish this task without feeling vibration in your nose, you are ready to move on to the next step. If you can't do it, enlist the help of a friend or a specialist. You may even need to find out if there is a physical explanation from a doctor.

When practicing, place your fingers on the bridge of your nose and make sure you don't feel any vibration on words that don't contain nasal sounds.

Practice These Sentences that Don't Contain Nasal Sounds:

- George liked his postcards a lot.

- Where will you go for your party?

- Yes, I did.

- I'd like a glass of water.

- You are right.

- Take the book to your colleague.

- Write the essay at your desk.

- Save your receipts for the right purpose.

- Sure.

- Which part do you like the best?

- Where did you go?

- How will you offer your services?

- Go to the post office for your box.

Make up your own sentences and say them without being nasal. You are well on your way to eliminating nasality!

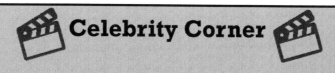

Celebrity Corner

Fran Drescher

Fran Drescher is well known for her use of excessive nasality. Listen to her as she speaks to Siri on the iPhone.

www.clearly-speaking.com/voice-branding-for-executive-leaders

Category: Voice

Subcategory: Quality

Glottal Fry

Perceptions of Speaker May Be:

- ☐ Older sounding

- ☐ Super laid back

Listener Reaction:

- ☐ May feel that speaker is annoying.

- ☐ Speaker's voice is grating.

- ☐ Speaker is difficult to listen to.

Category: Voice

Subcategory: Quality

Glottal fry (or vocal fry) is a problem associated with pitch. It sounds like a popping, crackling sound, and is typically present because someone is speaking at the bottom of their vocal range.

It generally occurs at the ends of sentences but can also occur on upward inflection. It can be very distracting but more importantly, it can be damaging to the vocal cords.

It is important to determine the frequency, duration and placement of vocal fry. It may require a specialist to help.

The common solution to eliminating glottal fry is to raise a person's pitch slightly or increase loudness levels. In addition, breathing properly without tension is part of the coaching course.

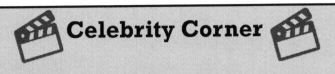

Celebrity Corner

Zach Hanks

Zach Hanks does a character, Thomas McCall in *Call of Juarez: Bound in Blood* that is low pitched, uses chest resonance, a southern dialect, is slightly monotone and has vocal fry.

On an NPR Interview with Serri Graslie and Anya von Bremzen, they talk about a special soup in Russia. It is also a demonstration of glottal fry in conversation. Both of them trail off with their voices and drop into a fry (a crackling, popping sound).

People with glottal fry have tension in their voice and don't use proper breath support. It is a difficult aspect of voice to self-diagnose. But everyone around the glottal fry speaker will hear it. CBS news did a story about it and can be viewed on the resource page.

www.clearly-speaking.com/voice-branding-for-executive-leaders

Changing Behaviors

A Final Note

Making changes in your vocal or speech behavior to reach personal or professional goals is not always easy. Knowing what to do and actually making it happen depends on your ability to make changes (time may be a factor), your confidence level and your motivation. For example, you might strongly believe in your ability to slow your rate of speech, but have no time to work at incorporating practice into your busy schedule.

Self-efficacy is belief that you have the power to reach a goal. If you have high self-efficacy, you are more likely to achieve your goals. To strengthen your self-efficacy, set small, achievable goals.

Success with smaller goals will improve your ability to reach larger ones, no matter what the goal you are trying to achieve.

The process of change involves three steps:

1. **Awareness**: You can't change any behavior without awareness that a problem exists.

2. **Conscious Level**: Intentional practice with a new, substitute skill.

> "You have to acknowledge a problem exists before you can actually go about finding a solution."
>
> **Demi Moore**

117

3. **Subconscious Level**: The new skill becomes automatic and routine in all conversational situations without even having to think about it.

There may be several situations that are tougher than others and the new skill may be difficult to maintain. These situations are often high stakes/high visibility situations. There are a variety of contexts and audiences that we encounter every day. You need to be aware of which situations cause more stress for you so that you can prepare differently for them. The situations that cause angst among individuals vary significantly from person-to-person. See below:

Low stakes: Casual conversation, Friends/peers, _____,

_____, _____, _____.

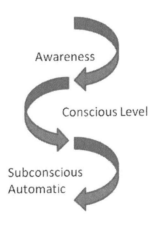

High Stakes: Presentations, board members, heated discussions, media interviews, _____, _____, _____,

_____.

Here are 10 tips to help get you started maintain a realistic approach to accomplish your communication goals:

1. Set realistic goals.

2. Plan ahead. Write down your plan and how you will benefit when you reach your goal. Set a beginning point and time frame for developing change.

> "Communication is a skill that you can learn. It's like riding a bicycle or typing. If you're willing to work at it, you can rapidly improve the quality of every part of your life."
>
> **Brian Tracy**

Make your plan visible so that you see it every day. Practice positive thinking and self-talk, or reminding yourself how your new skill will positively affect your life.

3. Write down the steps you will need to take to accomplish your goal.

4. Make a list of obstacles that might get in the way and remove them (if possible).

5. Talk about it with others so that you can get support and share your successes. It's motivating to have someone else care about your success and be willing to talk about it.

6. Give yourself rewards for making progress and for reaching goals. Even if you made progress on a small goal, feel good about this.

7. Track your progress. Short-term goals are easier to keep, and small accomplishments will help keep you motivated.

8. If you don't achieve your goal as you set out to, don't be discouraged. Look at the steps to your goals and see if you can break them down even more.

9. Write practice times down on the calendar. Even as little as 15 minutes a day of intentional practice can make a difference. After all, 15 minutes is more than you do now, right?

10. Stick to it for at least 21 days to make it a habit and 6 months for it to become part of your communication style. Your new style will become automatic in no time.

If this 10-step plan sounds overwhelming to you, you may not be ready just yet. You need to be motivated to make changes, but the ultimate responsibility falls on you to practice daily and be intentional about your changes. If you are ready to commit to making changes, you will!

Do not be discouraged if you don't seem to be achieving your goals at first; keep on trying until you get it. Remember, everything starts with baby steps.

"Life opens up opportunities to you, and you either take them or you stay afraid of taking them."

Jim Carrey

Section 4

How Four Clients Mastered Their Speech, Language, and Voice Skills to Become Successful, Influential Leaders

In this section, you will see a variety of situations and problems that clients in professional settings had with their speech, language, and voice skills. Of the hundreds of clients that I have helped, each client's situation is unique. For each person, there is a consequence if the behavior does not change. Often times, the consequence is directly related to the client's self-confidence.

Studies show that we are more likely to listen to and be influenced by a self-confident person. According to Lois Frankel, Ph.D., president of Corporate Coaching International and author of the bestselling *Nice Girls Don't Get The Corner Office*, "We make assumptions about people who exhibit behaviors of low self-esteem. We may ascribe lower intelligence, even though that's not true."

What does this mean in your career, if your customers and colleagues perceive you as lacking self-confidence? Will there be a loss of a sale? Will there be a loss of respect and credibility?

The following Case Studies are real people who had problems at work. Each person had been identified as high achieving individuals in their corporations, but their communication skills were holding them back. Each Case Study contains the following:

1. **Problem:** Each person had a unique problem to work on.

2. **Perceptions/Reactions**: There were often reported perceptions or reactions that the people working with the client had due to the client's communication style.

3. **Goals:** This section provides the goals of coaching based on the feedback from others, but also based on the client's values and professional goals. Significant time was spent on what needed to change in communication styles to align with the client's professional goals of who they wanted to be.

4. **Outcomes:** The outcomes are a result of the hard work the clients put into training to achieve their goals. It was a lot of work to attain a level of mastery at the conversational level but each client achieved this goal with repetition of the skill in low stakes conversations and tasks first.

Disclaimer

The names of the clients in this section have been changed to protect their identity and confidentiality. The types of problems that are in this section are extremely common issues that I work with every day. They are provided to help you identify with the common issues that many other people face.

Case Studies

30-year Old Marketing Director Increases His Credibility and Influence with the Senior Executive Team

Problem

Philip had a conciseness problem. He spoke too long, he spoke too much, and by the time he completed his message, he often missed the point. In fact, the audience didn't ever know the points he was trying to make.

Perceptions/Response

People complained that he dominated staff meetings and conference calls with too many irrelevant details. He was unable to persuade people about his ideas and had very little overall impact in most all of his interactions. He felt defeated and disrespected. Philip needed to learn how to say more with less.

Goals

The goal for Philip was to learn to be succinct 100% of the time. In order to make progress on his goal, Philip needed to understand his audience--what they valued and what was meaningful to them.

Armed with this new knowledge he could determine what information they wanted and needed to hear. For example, Philip's boss was a busy man. He valued his time. When Philip met with him, he knew that brevity was important. That meant that Philip needed to be crystal clear about his message to his boss so that he didn't waste his time. Not only that, Philip began specifically asking for the agendas of his meetings so that he could prepare his notes and know exactly what point he needed to make.

With an information sheet on every one of his audiences, Philip referred to it frequently. Before each meeting, he wrote out his objectives for the meeting and the information that he wanted to convey under each point. Then he worked on how to shorten each of these responses until it was concise and clear. Each time he spoke to them, he was prepared to give a message that would resonate with his audience.

Outcomes

By studying his audience and preparing his notes, he built stronger relationships with his team because he came across as really knowing and understanding them.

After preparing very diligently for a PowerPoint presentation and then presenting it, Philip enjoyed the many accolades he received from his peers about how clear and concise his messages were and how nice it was to end the meeting on time. Philip was amazed.

The next meeting was even more important. He was presenting to senior leadership. Philip decided that he would just make his points without any explanation. He thought that if anybody needed more information, they would ask. If someone asked him questions about any points, he was ready to give him a longer response.

Philip did exactly as he had prepared and only gave the bare minimum that was needed for these very busy senior executives. He did have to answer one question that he was ready to address clearly and concisely. Philip enjoyed getting back to his office and receiving emails from his boss, who said he had done a fantastic job. Philip said that he felt he had been influential.

• • • •

Senior VP Changes His Communication Style and Feels Empowered and More Self-Confident

The Problem

Donald was a senior executive in his firm. He had worked very hard to get to the place that he held in his organization. He was very smart, had a lot of business savvy and had a strong work ethic.

But Donald had difficulty relating to people around him. He frequently got criticisms from the people that worked for him because of something he was doing on a daily basis. Donald was sarcastic and condescending when he spoke to his direct reports. He didn't mean to be sarcastic and condescending. In fact, Donald was one of the nicest gentlemen I had ever met. Donald thought his sense of humor was funny.

Perceptions/Response

For those people who didn't know him very well, his sarcasm came across as being confusing; he left his listeners wondering whether or not he was serious or joking. This communication style was interfering with his ability to move forward in his career because people didn't know whether to take him seriously. This perception negatively affected his credibility. He had difficulty connecting and resonating with the people he was talking to and he made them feel uncomfortable.

The first time I met Donald, I was impressed with his clean look and his professional style. He was friendly, he smiled when I greeted him and he had a strong handshake, all of which made him appear very professional.

But when he opened his mouth to greet me and answer my questions, I noticed that his facial expression was flat and serious and his vocal tone was monotone. He made a few dry, sarcastic jokes almost immediately. Since sarcasm is sometimes used to put somebody down or to make somebody feel badly, it has absolutely no place in a work setting, ever, and didn't really have a place meeting me for the first time, either.

Donald's goals within his company were high. As a Senior VP, he had an opportunity to move into a Senior Executive VP position. In that position the conversational stakes were higher, plus he would have higher public visibility. In terms of his personal values, he wanted a style that showed compassion for the people he worked with and who worked for him. He believed in bringing out the best in people.

Goals

His desired leadership style did not align with his communication skills. He thought his sarcastic tone was funny and endearing. But once he realized that sarcasm left people confused, he wanted to eliminate this behavior not only in his high stakes conversations and his high visibility activities, but consistently in all interactions.

Voice coaching had three primary goals to build positive perceptions:

1. Work on a friendlier, warmer tone.

2. Learn to tell funny stories and jokes that were self-deprecating and illustrated the points he wanted to tell.

3. Develop a system for responding and presenting that was more direct and honest.

Outcomes

Donald worked hard on his goals and accomplished every one of them. The evidence of this was in the feedback that he received after a presentation he gave to his peers and direct reports:

> "Donald's piece was excellent—very simple message but the most inspirational. He didn't just talk at us but rather he inspired and challenged the senior leadership

127

team to do better – that we truly owe it to the employees within our teams to do better than we are doing today. Delivered with a sense of humor, but different from the others in that it was the most inspirational."

"Donald had a great connection with the audience!"

"I was particularly inspired by Donald's presentation and direct message!"

Donald was thrilled to get this feedback and reported that it was the best thing he had done for himself to improve as a leader. He said that he felt so much more self-confident and empowered because of the changes he made in his communication style.

· · · ·

Software Developer Slows Down His Speech and Everyone Understands Him!

Problem

Sidd was a brilliant software developer. His high level of technical knowledge was leading him on the path of becoming a director of his company. His aspirations were very high and he knew that he was on the right track. But there was one problem, at the managerial level, Sidd reported to various people including his direct reports, at staff meetings and to several bosses. Sidd didn't mind presenting at staff meetings so much but he noticed that people were clarifying information for him after he spoke. Additionally, Sidd had to repeat this message frequently. His native tongue was Hindi and even though he had an excellent grasp of the English language, he spoke extremely fast. Not only did he speak very quickly, but he also pronounced syllables wrong in certain words, which affected the way the word sounded. These errors made him very hard to understand.

Perceptions/Response

Sidd's intelligibility was moderately low amongst his peers, the people who reported to him, and to those whom he reported. When Sidd met people for the first time, his intelligibility was even lower. He recognized that people were not listening after a short time into his presentation. He knew this because of the questions asked after the presentation and how people turned to his American coworker to get clarification. Sidd didn't feel like he was respected or credible.

Goals

The overall goal of training was to improve Sidd's intelligibility so that he could speak fluently to senior executives and to be understood every time he opened his mouth. Training focused on the following:

1. Decreasing his overall rate of speech to the slower side of the normal speech rate range.

2. Help Sidd understand the rules of syllable stress so that he would pronounce words correctly every single

129

time, especially the industry words that he was using on a regular basis.

Sidd worked hard at his goals. He possessed all the factors that are needed for success in any coaching program. Factors that influenced the success of the program included:

1. A desire to make changes.

2. Motivation to do the work.

3. A good coach who helped him to identify development goals.

4. The support of the client's boss, who was asked to assist in ways that helped him develop and grow (If the boss is unwilling to participate, the work load becomes even more difficult for the client to achieve his goal.)

5. An understanding of the process and how making progress in a training program is directly related to the amount of time the person practices. It was essential to spend time practicing with intentional effort on the goals that had been identified every single day so that progress could be made.

Outcomes

Sidd was able to accomplish most of his goals in a short period of eight sessions. Work was still needed in the area of high stress conversations, but he consistently accomplished his goals in all other conversations.

Because of his improved speech intelligibility, Sidd was given new responsibilities at work that involved more communication opportunities. Three months post-training, he reported that he no longer avoided situations or people and felt confident about pronouncing words with the correct syllable stress. People at work and on the telephone were not asking him to repeat or clarify his message. He was even slowly incorporating strategies into stressful, highly charged conversations.

> "I've always considered myself to be just average talent and what I have is a ridiculous insane obsessiveness for practice and preparation. I strive to be like the greatest people who have ever lived."
>
> **Will Smith**

• • • •

Senior VP Eliminates One Little Word from His Vocabulary and His Credibility Soars!

Problem

George's speech patterns and communication habits were getting in the way of communicating effectively. His use of "you know," lack of eye contact, and the overall appearance of not looking "at ease" were all distractions to his message.

He desired a more professional, natural "look and sound" that showed he was in command of his subject matter. He was always looking for ways to improve and this time, his goal was to have more executive presence. He knew that if he made changes to his style, he would receive more support from the Executive Management Team.

Perceptions/Response

People in George's circles told him that he appeared angry and intimidating at times. His presentations were difficult to listen to because he had so many habits that distracted from his overall message. Since he had difficulty engaging his listeners, he wasn't as credible as he could be.

Goals

Speech coaching began and a Plan of Action was devised with the following goals:

1. Eliminate all word fillers--Use more pausing as an effective tool to engage listeners.

2. Reduce the speech rate.

3. Work on body language—chin up, eyes engaged with listeners, and good posture.

Outcomes

George was a quick study and he successfully mastered these areas in just a few short sessions! Here is what George had to report after a presentation that he gave following coaching:

"I just finished presenting to the Executive Management Team, including our CEO, and the Extended Leadership Team --a total of about 40 of the top leaders in our organization ... I nailed it ... No notes, good eye contact, with chin up, no ahhhs, soooos, or "you know," and at a relaxed pace. Thank you!"

With the few minor tweaks to his presentation style, he sounded like the topic expert that he was and was able to convey his message to his audience with much more credibility and influence.

Section 5

Powerful and Effective Speech, Language, and Voice Skills that are Industry Specific

In section five, you will find tips for specific industries. Every industry has its own unique set of communication skills that are necessary to be effective. In this section, you will learn specific industry challenges that exist for several groups (Finance and Marketing Executives, Professional Speakers, Software Developers/IT Executives with a Foreign Accent, and Professional Athletes).

Although most tips in all the sections are great tools to have in your personal toolbox no matter what industry you are in, the topics discussed are most important in each of these industries.

- Finance and Marketing executives often find themselves answering difficult questions. This section provides strategies to use when questions come up.

- Professional speakers rely heavily on their voices for their jobs. This article provides tips and tools to keep your vocal performance edge.

- Software Developers/IT Executives with a foreign accent have special needs around communication. Perhaps you experience frustration having to repeat yourself so often even though you have such a great grasp of the language. The reasons why you may be hard to understand are discussed. There are multiple places in this book to refer to for making changes.

- Professional athletes who are called on to give an interview after the game need to be clear, succinct, and humble. Use these tips to resonate with your most important audience—your fans!

Senior Finance & Marketing Executives

Handling Questions

Many emerging leaders and even seasoned leaders find themselves presenting more to senior management teams, and communication exchanges are more high stakes and high visibility conversations. This is very stressful for some leaders because it requires a different level of expertise that they may or may not be familiar with. In addition to giving more presentations, there are an increased number of instances where they will need to respond spontaneously to questions. Being unprepared to respond can be a credibility buster and career stopper! Feeling anxious and nervous about responding to questions is a common complaint. Here are some tips to help you respond intelligently and genuinely.

First of all, if you feel too nervous about how you are going to respond, you may not even hear the actual question. To make sure you understand the question and give the right answer, take the following steps:

- Long before you even get into a situation or give a presentation, anticipate the questions beforehand so that you can think about a response. Of course, you won't be able to anticipate every question, but you can try. If there is anticipated controversy and known friction, anticipating questions will give you an advantage for staying calm, cool and collected. You can also prepare for a question that comes up that wasn't anticipated. To prepare for this scenario, compose a preplanned generic response that may not answer the question, but lets the audience know that you are not avoiding a response, but will find out the answer.

- Take deep breaths to relax your body. Be aware of tension you have in your body so that you can use relaxation exercises on a moment's notice to help you relax. Deep breathing is an easy, quiet way to do that! Take a long, calm, deep breath before answering any question.

- When a question is asked, look directly at the questioner to improve comprehension of the question.

- Ask questions to increase clarity and demonstrate that you are listening.

- Pause to organize your thoughts. If you fear silence, you are going to need to practice this one. But remember that when you pause, you appear poised and in control. There is power in silence. Use this time of pausing to gather your thoughts.

- Repeat the question. Repeating a question has three benefits:

  - Buys you the time to think about your response.

  - You can take control of the question by rephrasing the question more positively, if needed.

  - Allows everyone to hear the question.

- Begin with a comment that resonates with the audience or the questioner. For example, "That's a great question, Lisa. I know that it took a lot of courage to ask." Or, "I have struggled with the same question and here is what I've come up with...."

- Choose one main point and support it. If you have the problem of having many ideas running through your head in response to a question, chances are you will have difficulty choosing a response. Try answering the question with the first thought that comes to mind. Then focus on two or three supporting points that tell a story. Let the audience know how many points you will cover, too. For example, "There are three reasons why I feel this way...."

- Give yourself 30 seconds (as a guide) to answer, or use no more than three to five sentences to answer. Let the audience ask you follow-up questions if your answer was not complete enough to them.

- Summarize for a conclusion. Once you have provided a succinct response, let your audience know that the end is near by saying, "In conclusion..." Then repeat the original question and a one-sentence summary. A mistake some people make at this point is to apologize or add on another piece of information like, "I'd be happy to talk about this more later." Add-ons are not necessary. Your response will be more powerful without it.

You never know when you might be called upon to answer an important question. Be prepared by anticipating questions as much as possible and then providing short responses that make your point.

Professional Speakers

Tips to Keep Your Vocal Performance Edge

At one time or another we are all guilty of taking important things in life for granted, and when we lose things, even temporarily, we really miss them.

If you are like most people, you take for granted a well-functioning voice for your everyday needs. If, you are giving a presentation, meeting a client or running a seminar, proper vocal performance is *essential*.

When you become hoarse or lose your voice altogether, you suddenly realize how important your voice really is, and how vulnerable your voice is to hoarseness.

The following list contains items that are necessary to maintain good vocal health. Generally, if you are consistent on just one item, you are not at risk as much as the person who does not follow any of the guidelines listed and has high vocal demands.

Let's take a look at your vocal habits. Which of the following activities do you do to maintain vocal health? Where do you fall short? Check the box if you are currently performing the activity.

☐ You drink at least 8-10 glasses of water per day.

☐ You pace yourself with regard to the frequency, intensity and duration of your speaking. Impose periods of vocal rest, especially on days when your vocal needs are greatest.

☐ You avoid chronic throat clearing, coughing and yelling.

☐ You avoid irritants of the vocal and respiratory tract like smoking, alcohol, drugs, etc.

☐ You maintain general good health including proper diet, exercise, getting enough sleep, etc.

☐ You use diaphragmatic breath support both for speaking and singing.

☐ You warm up vocally before a speaking engagement, including presentations or a vocally demanding day.

☐ You do relaxation exercises of the jaw, neck, and shoulders.

☐ You speak at your optimal pitch level.

☐ You monitor your loudness level, keeping your level at around three on a scale of 1-10.

How did you do?

9-10=Great job! You probably don't experience difficulty with your voice even if you depend significantly on your voice every day.

7-8=Good job! But you are at risk for developing voice problems depending on the amount of voice use. You may have
already experienced voice problems.

6 or Fewer=At risk! If you are a heavy voice user, you are most
likely to develop vocal fatigue or hoarseness.

6 Ways to Stay Hydrated

In the list above we talked about the importance of staying
well-hydrated. Good vocal hygiene (preventative care to maintain good vocal health) starts with good hydration. You will
lose your vocal performance edge if you are not well-hydrated.
Here are six tips to help you stay well-hydrated:

#1 Drink at least 8-10 glasses of water per day.

The benefits of drinking 8-10 glasses of water are vast! From
healthier skin, to removing toxins via your kidneys, to reduc-
ing the risk of heart attacks, drinking water is the "in" thing
to do!

For the vocal cords to operate efficiently, the elastic tissue,
which the vocal cords are made of, need lubrication. Good hydration gives them that lubrication. Moisture in your oral cav-
ity acts as a humidifier for your vocal cords. The human body
is an amazing natural humidifier! It's true, so long as you are
hydrated. If you have ever been really dry and thirsty, not
only is your entire body crying out for liquids but your vocal
folds are not receiving adequate hydration either.

#2 Get in the habit of taking water with you wherever you are.

Take frequent drinks throughout the day. If you have water with you, you are more likely to pull it out and drink from it.

#3 Avoid beverages that cause dehydration.

Certain types of liquids including carbonated, alcoholic, or caffeinated beverages should be avoided. Alcohol and caffeine are diuretics and actually cause you to lose more water. According to www.Gatorade.com, a good rule of thumb for checking your hydration level is to check the color of your urine. If it is pale (like lemonade) to clear, you are well-hydrated. If darker in color, reach for a tall glass of clear water and drink away.

#4 Drink even more water if you are traveling by plane.

If you travel frequently by airplane it is especially important to drink a lot of water because the air in an airplane is especially drying. The cabin air is less than 20% humidity, which has a drying effect in our nasal passages and throat. Fill up with water within 30 minutes before your flight takes off and request two waters if possible. Airports allow people to take empty water bottles through security. After security, you can fill up the bottle at the water fountain.

#5 Eat foods with high water content.

If that much water seems water logging, there are other ways to increase your water consumption. Eat foods with high water content: natural fruit juices, soups, stews, watermelon, milk, juice popsicles, and flavored water (noncarbonated). Sugared drinks actually rob you of water because they may lessen the absorption of water from the intestines.

#6 Keep a diary of your drinking habits for one week.

Record the amount of liquids you drink each day. It's the only way to know what you actually drink each week.

	M	T	W	T	F	S	Su
Water							
Juice							
Coffee/Tea							
Soda							
Alcohol							
Other							

Once you know what you are consuming, you can begin to eliminate one bad habit and substitute water in place of it:

- If you drink three cups of coffee a day, try drinking two cups instead and substitute a glass of water for the third cup.

145

- If you drink alcoholic beverages, drink equal amounts of water in between drinks.

- Substitute fruit juice for carbonated drinks and/or put a lemon slice in your water.

Your vocal cords will operate more efficiently and your body will run more smoothly just by adding more water to your day!

Good vocal hygiene is simple and necessary for optimal voice use and it begins by being well-hydrated! Now you *and* your vocal cords will be ready for your next speaking engagement.

Software Developers & IT Executives with a Foreign Accent

Why Am I So Hard to Understand When I Speak So Well?

You are bright, extremely intelligent, and a great asset to your company. Everyone raves about your knowledge and expertise. People ask for your opinion, yet they don't do what you have asked them to, or you receive a lot of blank stares. Although English is not your native language, you know you have an excellent command of English grammar and perhaps you've even lived in the U.S. for many years. However, you realize that people have a difficult time understanding you and you notice that your colleagues seem to be avoiding you.

How is it that non-native English speakers who have such a good command of the English language are still difficult to understand? There are six reasons:

1. Vowels and consonants are inaccurately pronounced, substituted or entirely omitted. Since vowels and consonants carry a lot of meaning to words, a substitution can change the meaning drastically. Some other languages don't use the same alphabet as English does, so many non-native speakers must learn entirely new sounds. Among the harder sounds to learn are /r/ and /l/. Vowels, if mispronounced, can also cause mis-

communications. Additionally, many English words are not pronounced like they are spelled. (This can create problems even for the native English speaker learning to say an unfamiliar word.)

2. Inappropriate stress is placed on syllables in words. Again, a non-native speaker will use the structure of his/her native language and apply it to English. Some languages don't stress syllables the same way that English does. In order to stress a syllable, we lengthen the vowel sound of the stressed syllable and we increase our pitch and our loudness on this syllable. Consider the following two words: thirty and thirteen. The first syllable is stressed in the word "thirty" and the second syllable is stressed in "thirteen." A non-native speaker whose native language gives equal length to all syllables is going to say these two words almost identically. Word meaning is carried in these stressed syllables in American English. When not stressed correctly or at all, the listener will probably not understand.

3. The rhythm and melody of speech (intonation) doesn't match American English intonation patterns. English puts stress on the important words in our sentences like verbs, nouns and pronouns. This gives the sentence more meaning. Say the following sentence stressing the word that is in bold:

- **I** like pizza, I **like** pizza. I like **pizza.**

These sentences are different based on the context:

- Does Sara like pizza? No, **I** like pizza.

- Do you hate pizza? No, I **like** pizza.

- Do you like chicken? No, I like **pizza**.

Some languages speak with very little intonation and so sentences sound flat. This interferes with intelligibility because American listeners are used to pitch variation to make sentences interesting and to give them meaning. English also uses a lot of pitch variation at the endings of sentences. Our pitch goes up at the end of some questions and down for other questions and statements. There are multiple variations of pitch that are used to help the listener.

If the rhythm of speech is broken up because the speaker doesn't link sounds in words or words in sentences, the resulting cadence of speech is choppy. It sounds unnatural and doesn't flow well. Learning to link sounds and words is a high-level skill that requires concentration, but is key to understandable speech.

4. The rate of speech is too fast. A fast rate of speech compromises the listeners' understanding, no matter who is speaking. Add mispronunciation of sounds, inaccurate stress, a flat pitch, and choppy rhythm and the speaker becomes especially difficult to understand. If the speech is too slow, it is difficult to listen to. Non-native speakers must be especially careful to speak at an appropriate rate that matches their speech and language ability.

5. The nuances and intricacies of the language have not been learned. /r/ and /t/ variations, contractions, word endings, etc.

6. Minor grammatical errors—although this most likely doesn't affect how well someone understands you, if you make grammatical errors your accent will be present.

Mastering these higher-level skills is key to successful communication. Here is a plan for you. Take one skill at a time and master it. You do not have to follow this order. The order at which you develop your skills depends on you ultimate goal. If you want to be more intelligible, you work on specific areas. If you want to sound credible and trustworthy, you may have to work on something else. If you are interested in eliminating an accent completely, you will need to work on all areas. If you are unsure about where to start to have the most impact for the goals that you have, get an evaluation from a professional who will provide you with the steps to take. Once you master a skill, cross it off the list!

_____ Word Endings

_____ Rate of Speech

_____ Vowel Sounds

_____ Consonant Sounds

_____ Melody of American English - Syllable Stress

_____ Rhythm and Cadence of American English
- Linking Words

_____ Grammar

_____ Vocabulary

_____ Subtle Intricacies of American English
(such as /r/ and /t/ variations)

_____ Voiced vs. Voiceless Sounds

_____ Contextual meanings - Understanding
Expressions, Jokes, etc.)

_____ Other (Volume, Nasality, etc)

Do you feel comfortable asking the listener for feedback? Many clients of mine tell me they like it when their listeners tell them that certain words didn't sound right. An adept listener will sometimes be able to point out the specific mistakes. One client told me that he was so grateful to receive feedback because the words that he had the most trouble with were ones that he frequently used in his industry. He went home and started to practice the words with his spouse. Soon, he was using them frequently and correctly in his conversations with other people. These are simple techniques that can have immediate effect.

"Being willing to take constructive
feedback may transform your life!"

Lynda Stucky

Pro Athletes

Speaking to the Media

You have won the game and the media is vying for attention from the star of the team! They know that your fans are patiently waiting to hear from you! What are you going to say? How will you present it? What is your best strategy? Too many times, a star athlete comes before the cameras and lets the fan down by being difficult to understand, not very likeable or unable to express themselves to or resonate with his or her most important audience. Here are some tips to help you prepare:

Attitude Adjustment

The audience will pick up your attitude instantaneously. Think about the situation and make a conscious choice about the attitude you want to convey. You are the voice for your team; how do you want to portray that? This is important for both losses and wins!

Being passionate about your topic is one way to show a positive attitude. The characteristics of a passionate speaker are vast. Energy and enthusiasm prevail. There is a lot of voice modulation and there is variation in loudness and speed. You may pick up on pauses where, after something profound has been said, the speaker gives you time to process it. Your facial and nonverbal cues are also present--wide eyes and lifted eyebrows, perhaps a smile and overall body energy that radiates to those listening. The transfer of emotion from speaker to listener is a common occurrence. This can only be done if the speaker feels conviction about the topic. You cannot fake passion, you must feel it to convey it. But once you do, your voice will take on characteristics that convey your passion.

The attitudes to avoid are arrogance, impatience, boredom, blaming and anger. Avoid expressing these feelings at all media interviews. Remember that it isn't about you (even if you were the star); it's about the audience. They want to feel a part of the team and they want to feel reason to be loyal and respectful. They will be forgiving (even if the game was a loss) as long as you are genuine.

Use Body Language that Is Congruent with Your Message.

a. Stand tall - Show your confidence with great posture. Pull back your shoulders; hold your head high.

b. Smile - A smile is a sign of likeability. It says, *"I'm friendly and approachable."* If you minimize your emotional reactions, you appear remote and cold. Of course, you wouldn't smile if the outcome of the game wasn't favorable. Then a solemn expression is more genuine.

c. Make eye contact - Look into the interviewer's eyes. It shows interest and openness to hear his/her questions.

d. Raise your eyebrows - Eyebrows play a powerful role in sending messages. Open your eyes slightly more than normal and raise your eyebrows to signal interest and recognition.

Enunciate Your Words and Talk Slowly.

If there is any place to use exaggerated articulation and a slow rate of speech it is on camera! Pretend that you are talking to an important family member and you really want that person to understand.

Use Simple Language

Use short, easy sentences. Compliment the fans, the other players and your coaches. A gracious player is a likeable player. Always use a conversational tone.

Take Responsibility

Be courageous when talking about a loss. It wasn't your teammates' fault or the fault of your coach. Assure the fans that there is work to be done and next time will be better. Humility draws others in and the words that you use will reflect that.

Congratulations!

You have made it through this book and hopefully, you have learned about the speech, language, and voice characteristics that brand us all. As a leader in your industry or emerging executive leader you can now align your speech, language, and voice skills with the person you want to be as a professional.

I wish you the very best reaching those professional goals, obtaining personal satisfaction and gaining self-confidence. May you find many great surprises along the way!

I would love to hear your feedback. Please visit our website, www.clearly-speaking.com or email us at lynda@clearly-speaking.com

Lynda Stucky

P.S. Don't forget about the Bonus Section with Zach Hanks that I have included. It's a great section, especially if you use the phone a lot in your career.

P.P.S. I've left you one final bonus on page 185 to help you instantly boost your confidence in less than 7 minutes – enjoy!

BONUS Section

This is a very special section on Zach Hanks, a gaming voice-over specialist from the games *World of Warcraft, Call of Duty, Mass Effect, Dragon Age, and Final Fantasy.* He gives a lot of insight about creating the right vocal sounds to convey meaning in the messages he must relay to his audience. He also has extensive experience with public speaking and offers tips and techniques to public speakers on conquering nerves and mastering material.

The benefits of this section include learning how to adapt an actor's style on the way that you communicate. We all have different ways of learning new information. There may be ideas from Zach that paint a clearer picture of the way you could possibly implement changes in your style.

> "What actors do is we don't focus on what we feel; we focus on what we are doing."
>
> **Zach Hanks**

Additionally, Zach's work as a voice artist provides us insight on how you can convey meaning when you speak on the phone. A voice actor has to convey messages and meaning without the advantage of visual cues. Speaking on the phone is very much like that same situation.

Finally, Zach provides first-hand experience of techniques for speaking to audiences. As an extremely experienced public speaker, Zach has had successes and failures as a speaker. He is candid about that and gives us all the opportunity to learn from his mistakes. He demonstrates that speaking is an evolving process that takes time to develop.

> "The 'pulling it off' point is where you start, it's when you know your lines, you know what you're saying, you've timed it, and you got it in under thirty minutes 'cause it's a 30-minute meeting. You're aiming for mastery, the kind of mastery Josh Waitzkin had at chess, that Yo-Yo Ma has at the cello, that Tiger Woods has at golf. You're aiming for mastery, and mastery is not about practicing until you're a great public speaker, it's about looking at your talk, looking at your presentation, and running it until it's second nature…"
>
> **Zach Hanks**

Zach Hanks

Captain MacMillan from
Call of Duty 4: Modern Warfare

Zach Hanks

This is a very special section that I am so excited to bring to you. In the summer of 2013, I attended a VASTA (Voice and Speech Trainers Association) conference in Minneapolis, Minnesota. There I met Zach Hanks. Now, you may not have ever heard of him but if you play video games, you have probably heard his voice. Zach Hanks is a voice-over artist who has casted, directed and voiced characters in nearly 80 video games including the hit franchises *World of Warcraft, Call of Duty, Mass Effect, Dragon Age, and Final Fantasy*. He has the unique opportunity of creating convincing vocal sounds and speech to convey meaning to his audience (with animation as visual cues). He also uses his voice extensively for lecturing at conferences and universities.

Voice-overs are very much like having a telephone conversation or conference call where there are no visual cues of the speakers and the listener relies heavily on only speech, language, and voice characteristics to convey meaning. Because there are missing visual cues, speech, language, and voice skills may need to be exaggerated if certain emotions or if the meaning is very important. For example, to be especially clear on the telephone, a slower rate of speech is necessary to be better understood, since the listener won't get the additional visual cue of reading lips. Pronunciation and diction also improve with a slower rate. To sound friendlier, being vocally expressive (more pitch variation), loudness, and rate may need to vary more to keep listeners engaged. Smiling while speaking on the phone can actually improve vocal tone even though the listener can't see you.

Below, you will find pieces of an interview transcription I had with Zach Hanks. I've included the most relevant pieces for you here in this book, however, if you are interested in listening to the entire interview (which I highly recommend), you can hear it here:

www.clearly-speaking.com/voice-branding-for-executive-leaders

How to Convey Emotion with Your Voice

Zach talked about conveying emotion to provide meaning to the script. He said that the old euphemism of "Fake it 'til you make it" applies here, but 'faking an emotion' and 'feeling an emotion' aren't as clear as people would have us believe. So, actors don't focus on feeling, they focus on doing. They envision the action. Here is what Zach had to say:

Lynda: You talk about the emotion and having to decide that emotion almost spontaneously, where they (the producers) say, "This is the kind of character; now let's see what you've got." And you've got to come up with the character emotion. Do you feel it or do you have to fake it?

Zach: Well, the phrase - the euphemism "fake it 'til you make it" really applies here, but the funny thing about it is that the line between faking it and feeling it is not as clear as I think some people think or would have us think. And I think the first thing that we want to do is, speaking as an actor, is that when we focus on an emotion or playing an emotion, I think we're doomed to failure because actors, even though we can reach a variety of emotions and reach emotional extremes in ways that seem beyond what a non-actor could do. If we really could control our feelings - I mean if human beings, actors or non-actors, could really control their feelings the psychotherapy and antidepressant industries would not exist. If we were having an emotional problem and we didn't like what we were feeling, whether it was sadness or grief or depression or rage problems or whatever, we wouldn't go to therapists, we'd go to acting class to learn how to change how we feel. So the notion that we can sort of change how we feel by attacking a feeling or creating a feeling directly is not possible in the same way that telling someone to not think of a pink elephant is impossible. As soon as you tell them not to think of it, it's the first thing they think of. If I tell myself, "Be happy, be happy, be happy," The first thing my mind does is goes "No, no, no, you're not the boss of me."

As David Mamet, the playwright and filmmaker, puts it, "The mind is ever jealous of its prerogatives." What actors do is... we don't focus on what we feel; we focus on what we're doing. We're actors, we act, we perform actions, we're not feelers who go and feel. I can't happy, I can't sad, what I can do is I can threaten, I can seduce, I can titillate, I can amuse, I can betray, I can attack. These are active transitive verbs; these are things that I can *do*. Now, when I invest in imaginary circumstances where the performance of these actions has very high stakes -

163

That is to say, let's say the grenade is flying into my foxhole and my action is to warn. I can do a low stakes warning: "Hey guys, there's a um-there's a grenade coming in," which is obviously absurd. Or I can invest with really high stakes and then we get somebody yelling, "Grenade!" at the top of their lungs. And I just act as if the stakes are real but what I don't do is play panic. What I do is I warn someone and I save their lives and mine with my voice. And it's about what I'm doing; it's not about what I'm feeling. And if I know what I'm doing and I invest it with the right- with appropriate stakes and I act as if those stakes are real. The emotion will - if all goes as planned - arise on itself. And I don't have to stop and think, "Have I felt the emotion?" or watch myself or observe myself feeling the emotion and then evaluate that I did it right because I felt it. Because if I'm watching myself, now I'm up in my head which is where I don't want to be.

Emotions are physical experiences, just like movements. So what I do is I turn to the guy in my foxhole and I yell "Grenade!" and I try to get him to get out of the foxhole and I do it behind the microphone. And that's all I do. And my body experiences the physical experience of the emotion. Adrenaline might rise, my heart will pound, my breathing will increase, and that's really all the feeling is.

Lynda: Oh, wow that is really interesting! It makes me wonder a little bit about some of the things that I teach when teaching how to have a friendly voice, for example. I give them a list of characteristics in speech and voice, and really it's manipulation of those speech, language, and voice skills that creates a certain sound. For example, if you want to sound friendly and warm you kind of lengthen your vowels, and you speak a lot slower.

Zach: Right, and for an actor what we do to get to that result of friendliness, what we might observe or describe as friendliness is we catch it in an action, and the easiest way to describe that is with active verbs. So we might say, "Soothe, soothe them, comfort them, reassure them." Because I can comfort you, I can use the words on the page to reassure you, but I can't "friendly" you. And if I try to act friendly, it's likely that I'm going to be a little bit more of a used car salesman, because I'm trying to put on something that's not genuine. But whether I'm feeling something or not - I can authentically attempt to comfort you, and hopefully get the response that I want in a person that's listening to me. So that's basically the actor's process of getting to, what I would imagine might be an equivalent result.

Lynda: Okay, so you're thinking that you framed it with the verbs, you said you do the active verb. Is that how you said it?

Zach: Yes, and that's the fastest way to direct an actor, and I would probably argue a non-actor as well, because it's ultimately the same thing. You have a goal in mind and then what you are going to do to achieve the goal. We can attack it technically, what we call the outside-in way of working, which is: lengthen your vowels, lengthen your words, extend the duration of your speech. I do work that way with actors, you especially when they have to yell, "Grenade!" They might say, "Well, I just can't go any louder." Then, I say don't go louder, go longer. Say "Grenaaaaaaaaaaaaaaaade," and draw it out. So, we can go outside-in and we can go technical; but we can also go inside-out and we can go - change your intention, which is to be heard and to be heard at a great distance and over the noise of gunfire. We can often achieve the same result.

Zach's style relies on thinking about and re-creating the emotion or feeling of a situation to come up with the sound of voice he wants to convey. This is just another tool to use in your toolbox when attempting to create your communication style. For example, what does it sound like when you soothe someone? In all likelihood, if you are soothing your child, you are sounding gentle, mild and comforting. That is a "sound," but it speaks nothing of the characteristics of the voice. For some people, this is a highly effective method of achieving the same results.

The Voice and Visual Image

Zach talked about how actors are often cast by the way they look and sound. Imagine Morgan Freeman playing a part that makes him look weak. It just doesn't happen because his voice is strong and powerful. Of course, for a voice over, you don't see the actors so it doesn't work the same way. Read this section to find out the correlation between physique and vocal image.

Lynda: I heard you on one of your interviews talk about how people see you for the first time after they've heard you and they find out who you are, and then they see you and they expect you to look like someone else. (Zach laughs.) My book is all about images and what we carry with our voices and how people judge us very naturally based on the way we sound. So I'm curious, what does that mean for you, what do people think you should look like?

Zach: Someone actually commented on the fact that I don't look like what they thought I was going to look like.

Lynda: Well, sometimes you hear a radio voice, you listen to it for years and years and then you see the broadcaster at some live event. This happened to me and it's amazing how I thought about someone the whole time that he was on the radio. Then when I saw him, he was completely different from what I had imagined.

Zach: Yeah, I think two great examples of that are the late Don Lafontaine, who was the movie trailer guy for a long time. We sort of the joked how he was the (Mimics Lafontaine's Voice) "In a world" guy and you'd look at him and you're like, "Seriously?" I expected him to sort of be 7-feet tall. Kind of like the joke that William Wallace (Mel Gibson), in *Braveheart* says, "You thought I was going to be 8-feet tall and shoot fire from my arse."

I'm 5'7" or something and what's funny about it is I haven't gotten a lot of "Wow, I thought you'd look different or I thought you'd be bigger," or whatever. I've gotten a little bit of it, but I don't look that outrageously different than what a voice like mine might sound like.

I've played masculine characters and maybe - they're usually in their 30s and 40s, I generally look like I'm in my 30's or 40's. I'm a reasonably athletic looking human being and I used to enjoy being in the weight room so, like, there's not a huge dissonance between how I look and how I sound. But one illustration of that phenomenon that I've experienced hasn't been sort of per-sonal, but it's been professional. And I've experi-enced it one with regard to sort of how I commu-nicate in my own voice and also with dialect; when I put on different dialect.

Lynda: Okay, tell me more about it.

Zach: Well, with regards to my own voice what I have found is that my type as an actor is just kind of how you come across and what type of characters you do. So let's take Dwayne Johnson, his nickname is "The Rock," he was a professional wrestler and he's also a popular actor; a huge, muscular guy and a strong, masculine voice. And so his type is obvious; he's an enforcer. You look at him and right out of the gate he is an enforcer, he is like Special Forces, he is obviously a pro wrestler, a body builder, he's a football star, he's a warrior. And those are the roles that he's played. And of course, then he plays comedic roles that are just dissonant with that. He plays a babysitter, and that's like - that's the gag. Like Arnold Schwarzenegger in *Kindergarten Cop*, he's a gigantic kindergarten teacher and that's the dissonance in the joke.

Now with me, my type for television and film, to me has always been very ambiguous, you see me and you go, "Bam! You're a heroin junkie, or you are a gangbanger. Or, you're the cop." You know you look at Chris Meloni and think, "You're the cop." Of course, he was also an inmate in *Oz*. Tom Hanks...*Every Man, Family Man*. Me, it was always really ambiguous and I couldn't figure out what the problem was. No one knew where to put me. In one episode, I was an assassin (in "Criminal Minds"), a victim, or a bereaved husband. So it just was really hard to peg. Then, I started doing video games and my type was obvious. So it was like my body, my face, my carriage couldn't figure out who the heck I was when you looked at me, but if you closed your eyes and heard me, apparently based on my casting, I'm a Marine. I mean, not the way I'm talking right now but when I put on the soldier voice that's what I am: I'm a Marine. (Marine Voice) "All right boys let's get this - let's get those sandbags up, let's get moving, we got conflict in the north."

I'm a Marine, I'm a chopper pilot, I'm Special Forces, I'm a Navy SEAL, and for fantasy I'm a warrior, sometimes I can put on an Ork but I'm mostly aggressive-masculine, hyper-masculine characters. But I'm not going to book roles in military films or as cops. So, that dissonance was a hindrance in film and television; for voice over, they never have to see me. And apparently, in my voice there's just no ambiguity, so that's been pretty cool.

As you process this section of Zach's interview, it's so interesting to hear how his "type" was not matching the TV roles he wanted to play. But once he removed the visual, his voice got stereotyped into a role. Ask yourself how important is it for you to look and sound the part that you wish to be as a professional. Is there dissonance between the way that you sound and the way that you want to come across? Are you aligned or do you need to adjust? Because dissonance will affect how believable and trustworthy you are.

How to Overcome Presentation Jitters

And about nerves....Zach speaks extensively not only for voice-overs but for the times that he presents publicly to audiences. He offered some great advice about dealing with nerves, what happens when we get nervous (physically), how he deals with his nerves and how to prepare for presentations.

Lynda: I'm going to shift just a little bit to the presentations that you do because I know you do a lot of presentations for conferences and also the lectures. That's what I work a lot with, with executives using their speech, language, and voice skills to develop them to their advantage. Do you ever get nervous when you speak?

Zach: I do, I do.

Lynda: You do. How do you deal with your nerves?

Zach: Well, the first thing is--my nerves are not crippling. I get them (nerves) but I'm not overwhelmed by them. I feel that I have the adrenaline in my blood stream and my heart rate has increased but it doesn't affect my work as much as it did maybe when I was in my early 20s doing my first professional audition, and my hands were shaking, and I was forgetting my lines.

Lynda: Yeah, so it sounds like you practiced and the more that you did it, that's what gave you the confidence. The nerves weren't as great as...

Zach: Yeah, I mean so part of it is having done it a lot.

Lynda: Yes, right.

Zach: Part of it though, is as an actor doing theatre – I have a mask to hide behind to an extent. Also, I know, unless I'm doing a one man show, the whole of the show doesn't rest on my shoulders; I get to throw the focus off of me, onto my scene partner from time to time. In addition, I know that I'm creating the illusion of another person. Like if I'm playing Macbeth, I'm creating the illusion of Macbeth; when they see me, they're not judging me, they're judging- If I'm doing my job right-they're judging Macbeth. Now when I'm doing my own material, like when I'm doing a lecture, a presentation, or I'm teaching, it's me. And that's much scarier.

Here is what I would recommend to anybody. First of all, the more you do it, the easier it gets. Two, figure out exactly what fear is: fear is an emotion and emotions are physical experiences. So, if you had a headache and you didn't want to have the headache, what would you do?

Lynda: I would take some medicine probably, Aspirin or something.

Zach: Okay. If you had an itchy rash, what would you do? You would use like a cortisone cream or something or some Benadryl.

Lynda: I was going to say some medicine. That was my first thought.

Zach: Well and that's the thing. If you were stressed out, you had a long day, you've been in traffic, you had an interview that went alright, and you're just agitated and stressed out and you didn't want to feel that anymore, what might you do?

Lynda: (Laughs) Do you really want to know? (Both laugh)

Zach: Sure! Well, you can give me - you can give me the acceptable answer or the real answer. "I would drink myself into a stupor." No, whatever you're comfortable with.

Lynda: Well, I do two things: I would either have a glass of wine, that's always relaxing, or I would go out and do some physical exercise, I would run or something like that.

Zach: Great. Well you sort of, in a way, you just answered the "How do you deal with nerves?" question. Now, I'm not going to recommend alcohol to people cause what's going to happen is people are going to have too much because the nerves are going to be so overwhelming that instead of having the one drink, they're going to have four. And then the alcoholic is going to use it as free reign to have eleven.

But the other thing: do some exercise. First of all you're burning off some of that adrenaline and cortisol. Two, you're taking charge of your heart rate and you're taking charge of your breathing rhythm and you're getting into your body. It's not fear like, a tiger jumping out of the bushes and it's just a mindless, thoughtless fear. But when we get to hang out in fear that is dread,

dread of something coming that we have some control over, but we don't know what to do and so we begin to have thoughts. We give credence to the thoughts. The thoughts are nonsense, the thoughts are babble. The thoughts we have when we're afraid are babble. "Oh, I'm not going to be able to do this. Oh, I'm going to suck, they're going to hate me." Whatever, it's just babble.

So, the first thing to do is to get out of your head, and that might be exercise: it might be doing yoga, it might be stretching, it might be deep-breathing or counting. It doesn't matter what you do- play the piano, sing, but get out of your head and get into your body. I've been terrified of playing music or singing, I used to do karate tournaments when I was in high school. I'm in a ring with an audience, fighting... That's crazy, that's worth being fearful over. But once it starts, I'm not afraid. That gets back to the whole actor thing: it's not what are you feeling but what are you doing. Think about that and the feelings will take care of themselves.

Now the other thing is: note what fear is. It's a physical experience. What is it? It's adrenaline in the blood stream, it focuses your mind on fleeing or fighting and that's it. You can't think rationally. It affects your nervous system, it shuts down certain systems, and it amplifies other systems, it affects your blood pressure. It affects your breathing depth, and breathing rhythm, and it affects your heart rate by increasing it. Your palms sweat. I get swamped in sweat. I get out there in a suit and I look like I was running a mile in my suit, and I feel and look ridiculous. But then I look at the situation, and look for solutions...

My heart rate is increased... How can I slow it?

My breathing rate is increased and more shallow... How do I deepen it and slow it down?

My blood stream is filled with adrenaline; my body wants to run away... What can I do with that?

The answer? Push-ups are your friend. Burn a little bit of that adrenaline off by being physical.

The last thing and this is the thing that people under-do and this is why actors can do theatre and knock it out of the park.

Lynda: I can't wait to hear.

Zach: Rehearsal, you rehearse. Young actors, beginning actors, rehearse to the point where they're able to get through it once without screwing up, that's what I call the "pulling it off" point and then they stop. They go, "Well I pulled it off, I'm ready." They're not ready. The point at which you're ready is something way farther down the road. The "pulling it off" point is where you start, it's when you know your lines, you know what you're saying, you've timed it, you got it in under thirty minutes 'cause it's a 30 minute meeting. You're aiming for mastery, the kind of mastery Josh Waitzkin had at chess, that Yo-Yo Ma has at the cello, or that Tiger Woods has at golf. You're aiming for mastery, and mastery is not about like, practicing until you're a great public speaker, it's about looking at your talk, looking at your presentation, and running it until its second nature and knowing that it's under time.

That's the other thing. If you have a 60-minute talk, you develop a 45-minute talk because if you come in under, they're going to love you for it. And if you omit material, they don't know because you didn't tell them you omitted it. They're not comparing it to what you could've done, they don't know what you could've done, they only know what you did. If you run over, or you have to rush, you're dead. So you rehearse and you rehearse and you rehearse. Whatever you think is over-rehearsing, do twice that much. And then, it's just like they say, it's just like riding a bike, you don't freak out when you get on a bike at 30 like you did when you were six, or when you get behind the wheel. That's the level of mastery that you want to achieve.

The last thing is perform it in front of another human being before your actual performance because being watched changes everything because it activates a part of the brain that has to do with self-consciousness and that part of the brain doesn't activate when you're rehearsing and you're on television. You need to have the experience of doing it while being watched, and then when you're being watched again it's the second performance and it takes the edge off.

Lynda: Those are great tips, absolutely great. And I love the way that you went into them with the aiming for mastery, I mean the rehearsal, that's something I always tell my clients; you have to rehearse, you have to practice, practice, practice. But I loved the way you described it, I think that is just so valuable, so great.

Zach: Yeah, I'm glad it's useful. Actually, a lot of it I learned just a few months ago.

Lynda: Really?

Zach: Yeah, I did some things differently for my VASTA talk because the stakes felt high. I was afraid of presenting the notion that vocal strain is just fine if it's worth it to you (if the payoff is worth the risk, like a stunt man or an NFL football player). If I presented it wrong, I was afraid I'd get run out on a rail. My initial drafts of the presentation that I was presenting were profoundly wrong. I re-drafted it for days, I mean, I took like a week and I just re-drafted it every single day until I finally was able to get my ego out of it, my fear out of it, my judgment out of it, and my need out of it and present it. I found a way to present it that was sort of insecurity free.

I also cut it shorter because I thought I had 45 minutes, so I tried to get it down to about 35. Then I took 45 minutes finding out that I actually had an hour. And that fifteen minute buffer was something I've never done. My first time talking at a conference I had an hour, and I got it in in an hour but I had to rush. The material was great, but I had to fly through it, so comprehension was low. The second time I did it, I did the exact same talk and it took me 3 hours to finish it. That's when I realized I had a 3-hour talk and I was doing it at triple speed. So, do 45 minutes when you have 60 and then you can relax and you're fine. Because needing to rush will make your adrenaline glands pump more and heart rate go up faster and increase your nerves.

Here is an outline of Zach Hanks' complete interview:

I. The process for studying and developing character voices

II. Adding emotion to the voice

III. Experiencing vocal fatigue—Zach's perspective may surprise you!

IV. Perceptions people have around his voice

V. Working with dialects

VI. Combating nerves for public speaking engagements

Again, if you would like to hear some of Zach's voice characters, you will find some videos available on the resource page:

www.clearly-speaking.com/voice-branding-for-executive-leaders

About the Author

Lynda Stucky, M.A., CCC-SLP is passionate about coaching mid-senior level leaders and emerging leaders on using their speech and voice effectively to establish credibility, position themselves within their company, and enhance their reputation as a topic authority. She provides training through one-on-one coaching, webinars, and the ClearlySpeaking Virtual Academy to reduce foreign and regional accents, and to teach speech and voice competencies to build a professional brand.

She is President of ClearlySpeaking, and is a certified and licensed speech-language pathologist. Her background in speech pathology offers unique skills for dealing with professional communication skills in the corporate world. She believes great communication skills are essential for the development of a leader and should not hold anyone back from achieving personal and professional goals.

When Lynda is not helping emerging leaders she is enjoying her garden and her yard, traveling to as many places as possible to experience new cultures, and enjoying physical activities to maintain fitness and good health. She is married and has three adult children and two cats.

Give Me 90 Minutes & I'll Transform the Way an Emerging Leader In Your Organization Sounds and Appears to You and Their Peers!

Like it or not, your emerging leaders are often judged by the way they sound – not just by what they say.

In today's business environment, the competition is fierce and the way your leaders communicate with your prospects, customers, colleagues and the media, matters more than ever – for both them and you.

What if you could help your emerging leaders feel more confident, sound more professional, improve their relationships with customers and colleagues, and become the trustworthy leader you need on your team?

Would you help them? Of course you would, and together...

We can help your emerging leaders align their professional goals with their speech, language, and voice so that their message is compelling, their conversations are fascinating, and your employees and customers respond positively to them.

How can we help your emerging leaders achieve this?

Introducing: 90-Minute Vocal Makeovers

In 90-Minutes, I can transform one of your emerging leaders, while showing your other leaders how they can help themselves.

There are 3 makeovers to choose from:

1. How to Boost Self-Confidence to Feel More Influential and Powerful

2. How to Eliminate Distractions So Listeners Pay Attention and Stay Engaged

3. How to Increase Clarity to Be Better Understood in Your Conversations and Presentations

For more details or to book a ClearlySpeaking Vocal Makeover, call me at 412-264-1717 or email me at lynda@clearly-speaking.com

Free Report Reveals:

"TWO Proven Speech Strategies that Get Peers & Leaders to Listen and Respect You Immediately!"

Dear Leader, now that you've read this book and know the 9 speech, language, and voice competencies to improve your communication and leadership skills, I want to gift you my special report entitled, "TWO Proven Speech Strategies that Get Peers & Leaders to Listen and Respect You Immediately!"

The first step to becoming a leader is getting people to listen to you. Then, to like you. Finally, to trust and respect you. This report (coupled with what you learned here in this book) will help you quickly speed up this process.

And, if that weren't enough, inside this free report you'll not only learn how to get your peers and leaders to listen and respect you, you'll also discover:

- 25 Characteristics Every Influential Leader Possesses
- 3 Competencies Every Executive Leader Has (and that you MUST master!)
- The 2 Surprisingly Simple-to-Learn Skills Necessary to Make It BIG (not having them sets you up for failure!)
- And Much More!

You see, when your peers and bosses listen and respect you, EVERYTHING CHANGES! I want that for you. This report can help – and it's free. Read it here now:

www.clearly-speaking.com/instant-respect-report

Made in the USA
Charleston, SC
13 January 2015